MOIST!

A Collection Of Erotic Sensations
BY MICHAEL GUINN

PARENTAL ADVISORY
MATURE CONTENT

Moist! A Collection of Erotic Sensations
By: Michael Guinn

Designed by: Michael Guinn
Editor: Anelda L. Attaway
Cover created by: Jazzy Kitty Publishing
Logo designs by: Andre M. Saunders and Leroy Grayson
Art design By Ms. Litza Boden
Photographs by: Michael Guinn, www.photobucket.com, www.zawaj.com www.scfnw.org, www.jamb.ca/mt/photos/2009/shallowwater.jpg, sebaspace.wordpress.com, and Photos from Various Artist via Web

© 2003 Michael Guinn Mental Massages Press
ISBN: 978-0-9892656-8-3
Library of Congress Control Number: 2014955837

All rights reserved. This book is protected under the copyright laws of the United States of America. This book may not be copied or reprinted for commercial gain or profit. The use of short quotations or occasional page copying for personal or group study is permitted and encouraged. Permission will be granted upon request. Urban Fiction, may contain strong language and content. For Worldwide Distribution. Printed in the United States of America. Published by Jazzy Kitty Greetings Marketing & Publishing, LLC dba Jazzy Kitty Publishing. Utilizing Microsoft Publishing Software. This book contains strong language and may not be suitable for children. Parental Guidance is suggested. For information regarding permission, please contact: Michael Guinn at (972) 704-5001.

DEDICATIONS

First of all, praises to the Most High for His blessings.

A heartfelt thanks to mom, dad and my brothers who I love dearly.

For LOVE, I thank The Love of My Life Shardel Brock Guinn.

For HOPE, I thank my children Gerald, Jordan, and Manaiya Guinn.

For FRIENDSHIP, I thank Marisa E. Pryor and Marion Mitchell.

For FAITH, I thank Spoken Images and the Fort Worth Slam Team.

For CREATIVITY, I thank the Zawadi Writers, of Dallas Slams.

For WISDOM, I thank The Fort Worth Poet and the Tarrant County. Poetry Community, Madden, Chris Key, Giselle, AJ, and Mike Hatcher.

A special thanks to Terry Moore, Fran Thompson, James Hawthorne, and the Sacramento Poetry Center, Ms.Nadia, Janean, and Anthony.

From my heart, a very special thanks to Ms. Litza Boden for her wonderful display of inspirational art. (Litza I bow to your vision)

TABLE OF CONTENTS

Introduction	i
I'm Sorry	01
About Michael Guinn and the FWPS Team	02
Mike Guinn Entertainment Photo	04
Moist (To Book Michael)	05
Quotes	06
From Love and Back	07
Photo of Mike Guinn	08
Stop Domestic Abuse!!!	09
Stop Domestic Abuse	10
Sh*t Just Got Serious!	11
The Love Jones Set	12
Lump	13
At Water's Edge	14
Walk a Mile in Her Shoes	15
Spoken Images	16
I Thought of You Today	17
Shades of Blue	18
Twenty One Pounds Ago	19
Pana-Remains	20
Special Events by M G Entertainment	21
3rd Annual Poetry Slam	22
I	23
One	24
Stormy Moments	25

TABLE OF CONTENTS

A Kiss	26
Faith	27
There	28
Fort Worth Poetry Slams at MIJOS FUSION	29
National Touring Schedule for Mike Guinn	30
That Night I Fell Into You	31
Stars Are Writing Poetry	32
If I'd Known	33
On the Inside	34
Pro-Men-Tum by Mike Guinn Ent	35
In Your Eyes	37
Butterfly Kisses	38
Violation.	39
New Beginnings	40
When a Man Cries	41
Chocolate Kisses	42
S.P.I.T (Spokenword Poetry In Texas!)	43
Giselle's Writing Workshop Poem #2	44
I'm Ready	45
The 10th Annual King and Queen of Erotica Poetry Slam	46
Moist	47
Love's Locomotion	49
Life-Mates	50
Love (Photo)	51
Shy Compliments	52

TABLE OF CONTENTS

Every Day 53
Photo by Ninah Dee 54
Photo of Mike Guinn Performing Spokenword 55
The Taste of Touch 56
You Should Have 57
At Lovers Rock 58
Beautiful 59
A Poet 60
Paralyzed 62
My Favorite Flower 63
Candlelight Reminds Me 64
Mourning 65
That Island in Your Eyes 66
Size Does Matter 67
Imagination 68
Centric 69
Stop the Violence Against Women 70
Beginning of the End 71
Boo-Ku's 72
Of Seasons Before 73
Afterthoughts 74
All of You...Haters Can Just Kiss My Couplet 75
Chosen: A Letter to My Soul Mate 76
My Secret Little Fantasy 77
Giselle's Writing Workshop Poem #4 78

TABLE OF CONTENTS

Giselle's Writing Workshop Poem #3	79
BUSTED	80
Shades of Day	82
Without You	83
Shattered Glass	84
A Stranger in Your Eyes	85
I Wish a Motherfucker Would	86
Babe	87
Blue Interludes	88
Sleep	89
Shallow the Water	90
Love's Jambalaya	91
Introducing National Poet-Author-MC-Mr. Michael Guinn	93
I Dare You	94
An Angel's Halo	95
May I	96
End Domestic Violence	97
Photo of X Blu Rayne and Mike Guinn	98
The Color of Misty Blues	99
Silhouette	100
We Made Poetry	101
Insignifiny	102
Chocolate Covered Fantasy	103
What the Hell You Doing Online?	104
Tongue Foo	105

TABLE OF CONTENTS

Giselle's Writing Workshop Poem #1 by Mike Guinn 106
Reeses Peeses 107
Skid Marks 108
Minutes-Hours-Days 109
Please Say Yes 110
Stolen Glances 111
Love Jonz Presents "Addicted" 113
Now Booking Youth Mentoring-Power Poetry 114

INTRODUCTION

This volume of work is an unrequited reflection of the joys and pains from life's lessons and loves lost.

It is a journey from the corner of my soul to the bottom of my heart through the corridors of my mind then back again.

I want to share the story of my life through poetry with you.

ENJOY!!!

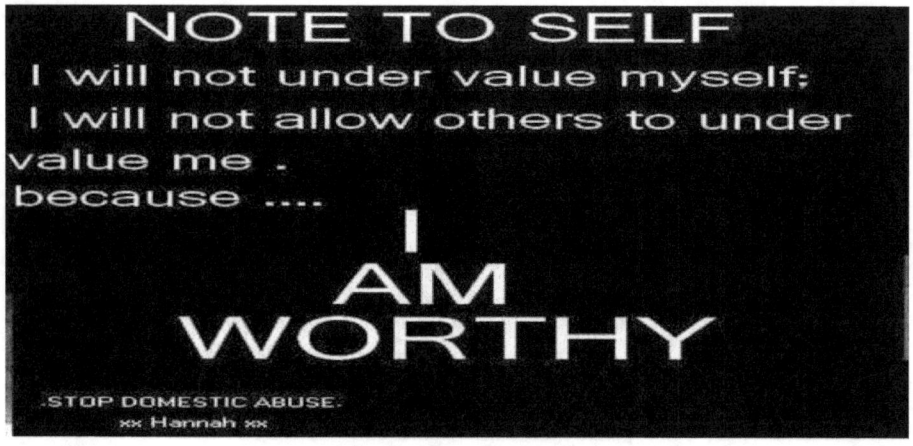

I'M SORRY

Someday...I'll write a poem that wins the Nobel peace prize for the peace I couldn't find in your eyes.

You...be that poet, writer, sole survivor and your misery cuts through me...truly...taking me back to that moment in your story where you first lost your glory.

And I can only imagine how it must feel to have wings and not be able to fly.
That has to be the most painful feeling any woman could bear.

Well...I've never known that feeling. I've never felt the sting of words without wings become dirty pretty things. And I've never screamed at the top of my lungs and had no one hear my cry. I've never known what that was like. I've never known.

And even though I've never been where you are, I can still feel the scar on your spirit. Cause when you speak...I hear it. And even though I've never had hopes bashed...I can still hear the echo of dreams smashed like a thousand fist against the window of your past.

But...I...have had words trapped like Lacey's Verbs...dying to get out and had doubt... just beat them back down until they became poetic lumps in the throat of my soul.

I've known...what **THAT'S** like! I've known!
But tonight...I **REFUSE** to let you stand there all alone...wrapped in blues, clutching black, seeing red.

YOUR VOICE...WILL NOT BECOME SIGN LANGUAGE FOR THE GHOST OF YOUR ANGUISH! BECAUSE TONIGHT! YOUR...WORDS TAKE FLIGHT! THEY SOAR! Traveling from metaphor to metaphor, giving life to incomplete sentences! THEY SOAR!

Stretching the limitations of sound, YOUR words fan the clouds and cool the sky...They Soar...Capturing the moment...They Soar!...Freeing the soul...They Soar! THEY SOAR!!! And...I just wanna say...I'm sorry...sorry for every man who never said HE was sorry.

Sorry...for all those times...your essence was left dying in the shade of never...forever road kill for vultures...too stupid to see...that in your eyes blooms the seed of their culture. Sorry...for all those nights your heart was left tangled in the curve of a smile as crooked as his shifty grin...To me THAT is the greatest sin!

And I want you to know that the prize between your thighs could never match the beauty inside your eyes...because you are beautiful. And I PROMISE to never disrespect you with fist, this...or this...Just protect you with this, this and this...

And I know you may not believe me, I know...but...tonight...I'll take that chance to say...I'm sorry.

ABOUT MICHAEL GUINN AND THE FWPS TEAM

Michael is a Texas native who holds a Masters Degree in social work. What he witnessed as a caseworker for Child Protective Services is what inspired him to begin writing poetry and spoken word. Since then he has become one of the nation's top advocates for social justice using the art of high-powered poetry and spoken word performances for awareness. He has received national acclaim for his highly interactive creative writing workshops and is the premiere Spoken Word Open Mic Promoter in Texas.

Michael is a 3-time National Poetry Award winner. In 2009, he was named Community Mentor of the Year for his advocacy for domestic violence prevention.

In 07'Michael placed 7th at the National Poetry Slam Championships, 4 time AIPF Slam, 06' winner and runner-up at the Arkansas Grand Slam, 08' Omaha Grand Slam Champion and appeared in the highly successful Poetry and Pose Fashion show with Eva Pigford and Keke Wyatt. He and his teammates consistently rank among the top national and international poets since they began sharing their soul in 2002. The Fort Worth National Poetry Slam Team has been ranked as high as #3 in the country. Members of this incredible group of poets have placed or won awards at almost every level of performance poetry competitions. He has opened for Russell Simmons, Malcom Jamal Warner. This includes the Akoben Word Festival, Austin International Poetry Festival, Toronto International Slam Championships, (Co-Champion) 2 time national poetry slam finalist. Arkansas Grand Slam and Bluebonnet Poetry Slam just to name a few. Michael and other members of FW Poetry Slams have performed all over the country and parts of Canada (Toronto Music Festival) and are some of the most sought after spoken word artists in the nation. Michael has successfully promoted four Hollywood Films, been in countless commercials, plays, short films, documentaries and numerous publications. His dynamic delivery and energetic performances have put venues on the spoken word map. They've worked as a lead actors as well as appeared on television, magazines, radio and internet ezine globally.

WORKSHOPS Mike Guinn host **"The Workshop"** a performance poetry workshop that addresses bullying, suicide, depression, education, and other issues that plague our society via an intense focus on emotional literacy.

Michael Guinn's leadership has ignited the spoken word community in the Dallas Fort Worth area by continuously holding consistent and poet friendly open mics and competitions every week. Affectionately and appropriately dubbed.

ONE OF THE HARDEST WORKING PERFORMANCE POETS IN THE WORLD! Michael is the leading performance poet and creative writing workshop facilitator in Texas and his vision has driven him to author more than ten poetry chapbooks, DVDs, Anthologies and numerous spoken word CD's. He is a teacher, social worker, motivational champion, mentor, and a voice for all.

Find out more about Michael by visiting www.mikeguinn.com or email us at jordanmichaelg@yahoo.com.

To Book Contact Michael at (972) 704-5001, Personal Cell (972) 704-5001, or Fax (972) 438-8986. Find Michael on various social networks such as www.mikeguinn.biz, www.meetup.com, www.facebook.com/mikeguinn1, **https://twitter.com/#!/jordanmichaelg,** www.coloredpeople.net, **or just Google Mike Guinn Poet.**

MOIST

WET SINSATIONS BY MICHAEL GUINN

*To Book Michael
Simply Call (972) 704-5001*

*Is available for private performances
www.mikeguinn.com
www.twitter.com
www.meetup.com
www.cdbaby.com*

Quotes

*"I have a dream that one day, my father's fears,
my mother's tears won't drown in the screams of forgotten years.
And tomorrow's sun reappears with the dawn that rises here."*

Michael Guinn

"Before attempting to comb through hairs of wisdom, one must first massage the scalp with knowledge."

Michael Guinn

Copyright 2003 Mental Massages Press
Michael Guinn–President/CEO
All Rights Reserved

There's nothing sexier than an educated woman

From Love and Back
Letter from the broken hearted

I've almost recovered…
I'm almost there, so beware…

It's my fault you see, because that's what happens when you make someone your world. You lose yourself and you can't see them for who they truly aren't and never were. And love becomes a blur.

Now I'm stuck dodging the dilation of her pupils, searching for the poetry in her eyes. I'm scratching for an existence with the persistence of a weed but now I concede. Because I'm bleeding torment, spitting up words, crying rhythm. And all I want right now…is for her to feel this pain, I want that shit to hurt, I want it to feel as if someone has cut a slice of her soul away. Because that's how I feel…inside.

I'm still stuck here…dangling on tear ducts, about to erupt.
Optically aroused but confused because I feel used every time she's near.

I may not have much hair on my head but on the inside, my love grows like an afro.

I may not have the soft skin she desires but my love is smooth like lotion.
I may not be young but my heart is forever evolving like fortune's child.

If she knew how much my spirit weeps for her…she allows herself to fall into love with me. All over again…

But all I can do now is hope that someday, when her body stops racing to fill in the gaps between her thighs. Maybe her eyes will open and for the first time, allow her mind to catch up to the emptiness inside her chest.

One day…perhaps she'll rest and see me standing in the shadow of her perception with open arms and come back to me…

But for now she's preoccupied with that wet piece of pride hidden behind that well groomed jungle between your thighs…Her Queen Dom cum.

And soon it'll be too late to realize that there's a soul there…there's a soul…And if she'll just go back and begin to pick up the pieces, sooner or later she'll know what love is!

But it won't matter…because it'll be never be enough for me.

STOP DOMESTIC ABUSE!!!!!!!!!

YOU CANNOT HEAL A LIFETIME OF PAIN OVERNIGHT, BE PATIENT WITH YOURSELF, IT TAKES AS LONG AS IT TAKES TO REBUILD YOURSELF

"It is better to have an **ENEMY** who honestly says they hate you than to have a **FRIEND** who's putting you down **SECRETLY.**"

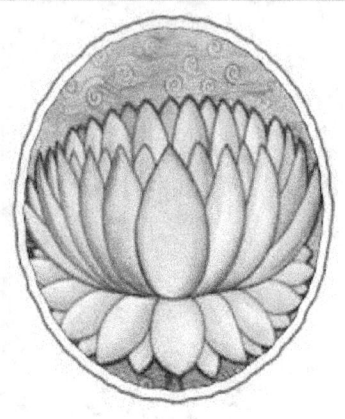

STOP DOMESTIC ABUSE.

The Lotus Flower is a symbol for courage, purity, and awakening, and it mirrors a survivors' journey towards healing and recovery. Like the Lotus Flower, survivors have been at rock bottom but have risen to show their strength, their worth, and immense courage, and their gracious beauty.

Courage doesn't always roar. Sometimes courage is the quiet voice at the end of the day saying, I will try again tomorrow.

trust takes years to build, seconds to break and forever to repair.

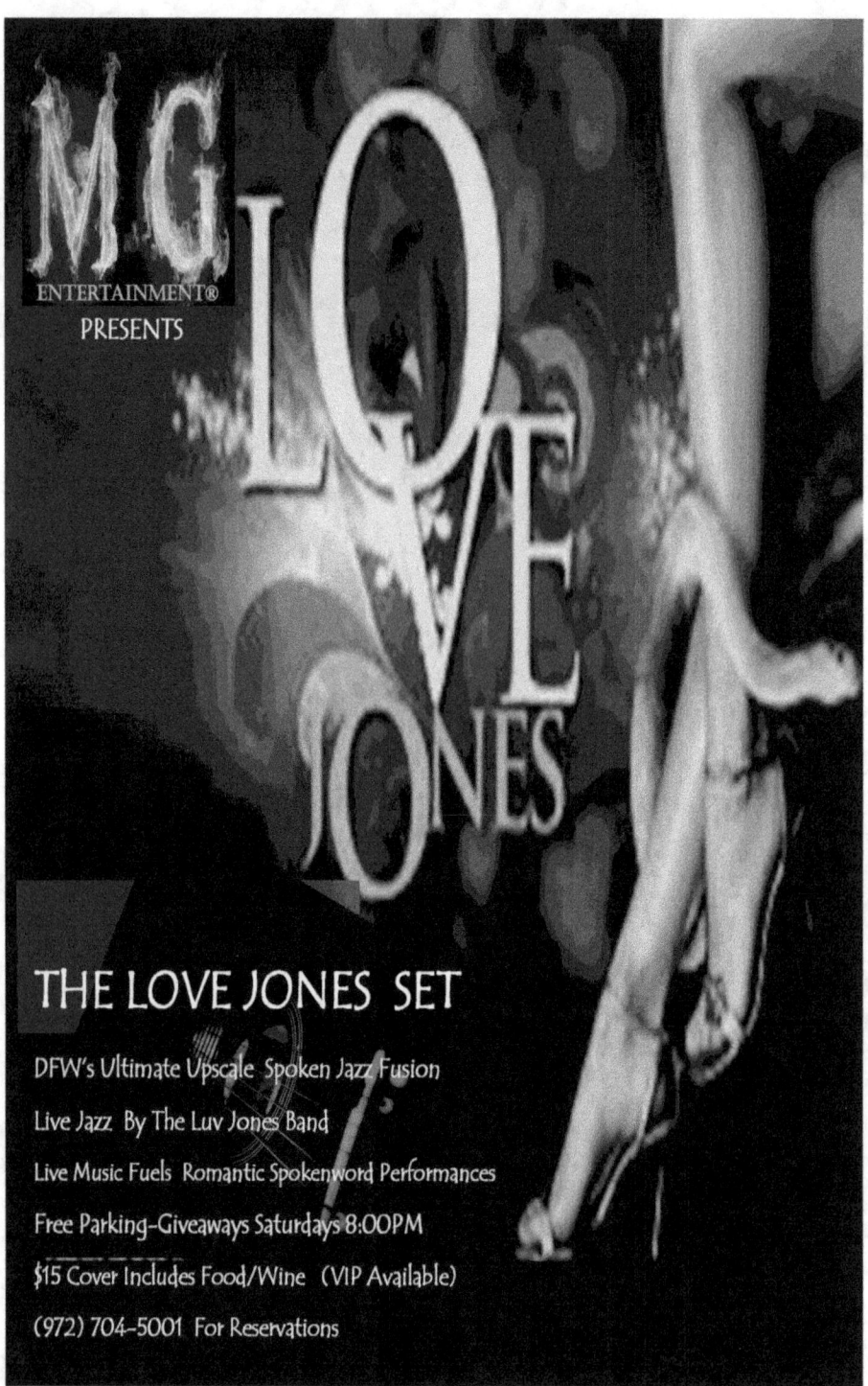

LUMP

Her name…was LULA MAE but her people called her…LUMP!
Now...Lump...stood 5'8 weighed bout 170 pounds with ass for days.

She had a tight little old package if you ask me. Of course...I'm no expert at picking pretty women ya know. But this one...was FINE!

Her lips, were kinda cracked with breath like funky ass cheetos
And she spit when she said words like "punk" or "bitch"
Ahh such a sweet academics…from a ghetto genius.
Y'all this gurl…was fine!

She had no eyebrows, wore green contacts with a pair of 99 cent shades perched way up high on that big ass forehead.

She sported a purple nose ring, which went well with her multicolored ear piercings and a stylish imitation gold chain, already turning shades of cheap.
But y'all let me tell ya…THE GIRL WAS FINE!

Her hair was no more than an inch high, dark red with blue streaks
Cut in a country fade with naps and buckshot's in the back.

Her toenails, chipped, crusty, curled up little claws which matched the dents in 5 of her 10 remaining teeth.
Oooweeeeee! I'm telling ya this girl was fine.

She wore knee highs up to her thighs
A faded blue jean skirt and flip-flops, which
Complimented that loud ass turquoise halter top
She knew how to shop. But let me stop
Cause this girl...was…fine.
Sometimes while sleeping, she snored like a Russian racehorse
Smoked black and milds, dipped skoal and cucumbers and I wonder
Why she wasn't married by now.

During sex. She fart and snort like a pregnant hog and say romantic things like "My draws stuck up my butt" "Get off me punk" or "Don't make me cut yo ass nigga"
Ahhh such sweet sweet words from an absolute angel
Now, y'all can't tell me I don't know how to pick em…
Cause this girl fine.

At Water's Edge

I my dreams...
I become lost as I toss and turn in this yearn I feel for you.

I awake to the touch of your breath on my cheek and I...can no longer sleep.

I imagine your lips becoming this luscious springboard that catapults me into eons of desire, suspending my fragile emotions from Jupiter heights just moments before releasing me into the destiny of your eyes. I've never fallen so far.

I clutch chagrin as love engulfs me in an endless ripple from waters I've never known.

But I seek more than just a midnight swim in your moonlight,
I want more than to splash in the waves of your warmth,
I need more than just a sip of your sunshine.

So I'll...hold my breath and began this improbable journey
   which begins with a plunge into passion...
      as I surrender to sensuality,
         submerge my spirit and swim soulful seas in search
           of your poetry.
              And my journey will not end until I reach
                the romantic revelation that rests
                  At Water's Edge.

The Dallas County Sexual Assault Coalition
Walk a Mile in Her Shoes®

The International Men's March to Stop Rape, Sexual Assault & Gender Violence

I Thought of You Today

For J.

For the second consecutive night, I've awakened at 2 am.
Got in my car, driven to San Fran, felt the sand and watch the sunrise inside my eyes.
You see...I thought of you today...

As I walked that lonely beach, each step left footprints filled with teardrops that became images of you.
I watched you wink at me, your smile, your laughter and I found myself running barefoot, chasing sea gulls...just to keep up with the moving picture that your memory had become.

You were a silent cinema stretched out across the shoreline of my mind rewinding the good times we once shared. Your whispers echoed like seashells, your eyes shone like moonlight, your breath moved like trade winds.
I felt your presence and smiled, because for a brief moment...I had you again.
You see...I thought of you today...

And as dawn approached, your face quickly faded into time bubbles bursting from the prick of reality. And no matter what I did, it was simply not enough to sustain the love I'd come to adore and I missed you that...much more.

And as your essence disappeared in the distance...I fell to my knees and tried to recapture the magic of loving the you, you use to be...the you that use to see...me... as the love of your life.

I tried to grab your image from the sand but your face turned away and left me cold. And I wondered how could my arms be so empty for what my heart still holds.

My body collapsed and my face dug deep down in regrettable retreat as my eyes closed and I cried my heart out for the millionth time.

The salt from my tears mixed with the sea and heartache's waves washed over me like God's cold blanket...and I thought... this must be where tears go.

Because I've cried an ocean since you've left...I mean...for me...it will always be this way...because you see...I thought of you today....missed you last night and needed you tomorrow.

But I suppose God still has some work to do...because no matter how hard I try or how much I pray...I just can't stop loving you.
So...I just wanted you to know...that I thought of you today...I always do.
And where ever you are or will be...I hope that you...thought of me...too

Shades of Blue

My mother, earth
 My father, time
  Brother winds
   Sister rains inside my mind
    Their frown, my moon, their smile, my sun
     Here together we live, together as one

         I've been dreaming in shades of blue again
          Misty colored memories crystallize upon my cheeks
           Like diamonds in the rough
            And hope becomes a collage of cold moods
         I'm dreaming in shades of blue

So strange mankind
 Painted in tints of summer shadows
  Tethered by winter gray shades of torment
   Spewing hate like crimson vines
    While precious seconds become insects eating away at time

         The elimination of my imagination
          Visions and interpretations
           Causes me to cry in colors
            Because we're still unable to love one another
             And the sting of tear drops stain as life becomes smothered

But these words are just words
 Defined by Words that Curse Words
  Confined in an evolution of time
   Revolving in a revolution of sound
    Evolving in an evolution of moods

 And we are left dreaming in shades of blue.

Twenty One Pounds Ago

Only God knows or cares what happens when I walk out that door.

All I know is
21 pounds ago, I was happy
Now I'm just a sad bag of confusion
Losing my mind, trying to figga whether
I should pull the trigga on my reality.

Let the Devil take my soul
21 pounds ago TODAY, I LOST CONTROL.

There are memories that still haunt me
Hell nobody sane wants me.
The scars from love and war
Just aren't becoming

My perception of her deception is a reflection of my faith
I have none, just a sun that sets way too late

My definition of God's wisdom is a jaded cataclysm
A faded inscription, man's depiction of some old time religion.

Sometimes I believe living is overrated.
21 pounds ago TONIGHT MY SPIRIT MIGHT HAVE MADE IT.

You see there is no hope in my future
Just a heart full of sutures
Patches of then, way back when
I didn't feel like such a loser.

So if this sounds like good-bye
Then baby, so shall it be.
21 pounds ago tomorrow
There was a poet
And I was HE.

PANA-REMAINS

For J.

She was a phenomenal woman…but she's gone...told me she needed to see where she wanted to be...and Right Now I feel as helpless as an abandoned child in the middle of I-30 during rush hour dodging little silver Hondas switching lanes on their way to hotter springs.
I can't eat, I can't even sleep, all I can do is roll over and hope that life slows down long enough for me to learn to walk again.

But how can a man be strong when all along what he thought was right was wrong. How can someone just start a fire, without fanning the flames and then abandon a burning desire GOD…you tell me how could you let them do that…to a good man.

Tell me how can a heart so empty be so heavy
So heavy that it cuts off the circulation to veins, killing membranes with strains that link into chains of pain…and all that's left are just "PANA-REMAINS"

Oh I've tried a little bit of everything.
Aroma therapy…but all I could smell was her.
Art appreciation only reminded me that in her eyes my value had depreciated.
Tried alcohol...but you can only drink so much Riunite Lambrusco
Before drowning in sorrow. Because without her there was no tomorrow.
And that…that unbearable silence where once were the beat off two hearts, slowly smothers me, I'm choking, I can't breathe because what I thought I needed I could no longer have…at least not in this lifetime.

If only I'd seen the signs or had some training on how to recognize love's disguise. Somebody please tell me what good is my Master's Degree when I can't even master…me.
I'm trying to be a man tonight…Lord knows I am.
But I'd be lying if I said it didn't hurt…and I've already cried a river LANGSTON.
Because I was dying inside…and I'm still dying.

If only she'd stayed around long enough to see her seeds sprout spirit leaves, bearing love's fruit on these life-limbs. If she'd just talked to me and told me what she truly needed…I would've done anything…I would've given my soul…because I loved her more than me…I just wanted give her my all.
But it's alright because I live and learn to hold my head up again.
Learn to like myself and for the very first time I learn to love me just the way that I am...even if I am without her. But that night was the night the poetry almost died…taking with it a part of my desire…that I was barely able to find. That's why I didn't write for a while.

Because you have to have a love for what you do in order to keep on doing it.
I guess that's why she left. For now...this is all that remains of my heart.

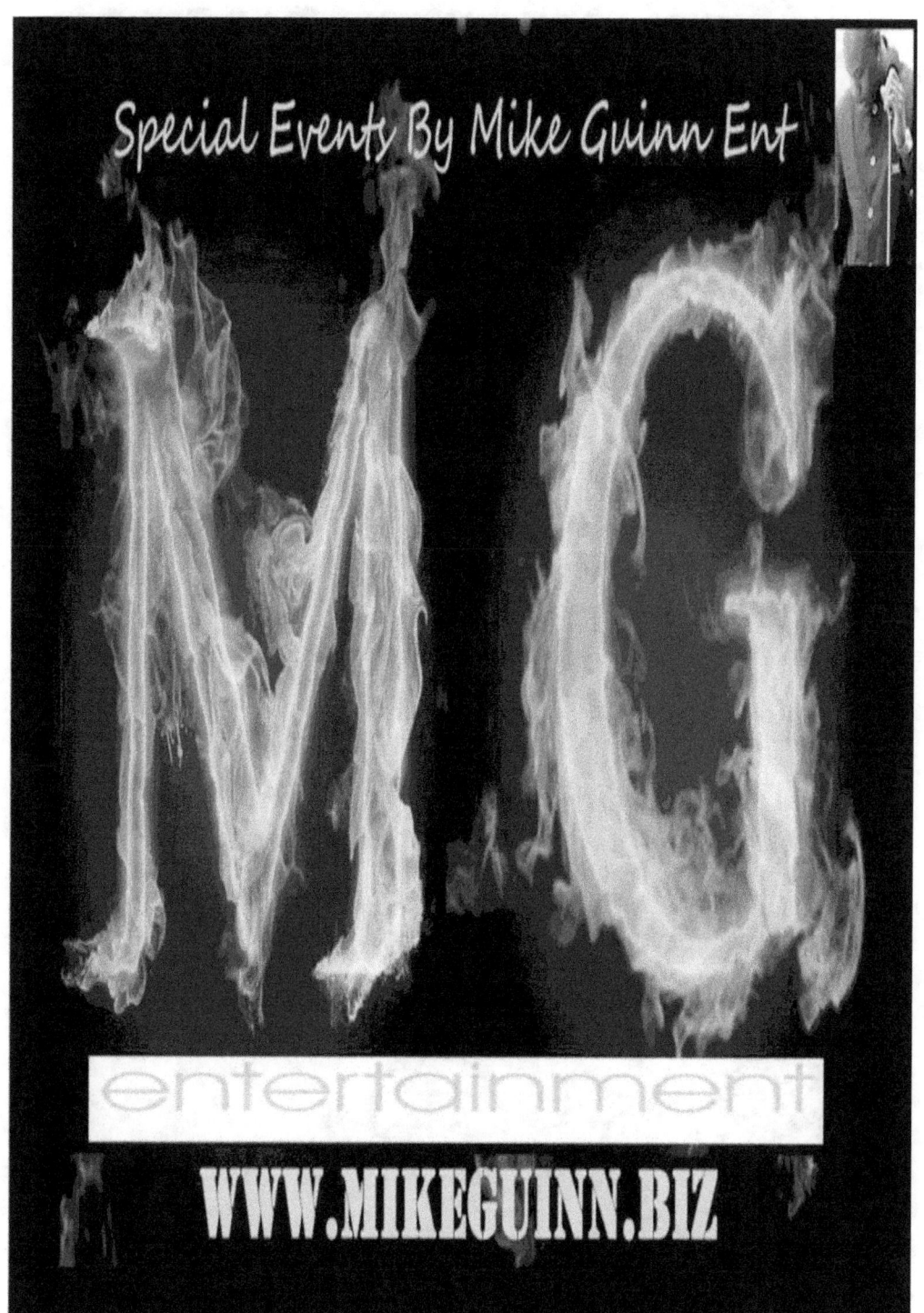

I

I
Come to you
Bare
Naked
My emotions all but exposed
But here
I am
I
Come to you
Half of a whole
That has no half to hold
But still
I
Come
To
You

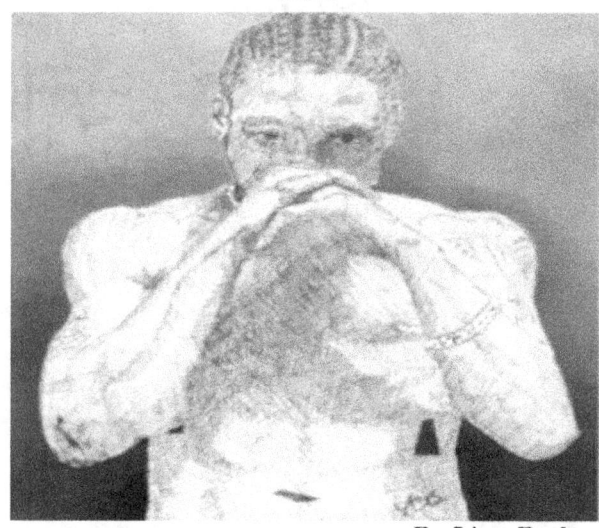

By Litza Boden

ONE

Somewhere near the end of time
Tears wash away stains
Left upon the fabric
Of our souls

Freedom flows freely
Dreams and life meet for the first time
And we become One

We become one you and I
Humble
As we stumble
In and out life's jungle

But still
We
Remain
as
One

Stormy Moments

As I listen to the falling rain
I close my eyes and watch tiny naked Pygmy women dancing
near a waterfall of sound.

This moment creates a stream of free flowing rhythm
that chases the tide of my life
and I realize that I'm crying inside.

The thunder so loud and frightening
reminds me of the stormy times
and how much I miss the sunrise in your eyes,
still morning denies my escape to the next day.

As I breathe in silence
I inhale the freedom hope brings
exhaling the Stormy Moments that remains.

Art By Litza Boden

A Kiss

It's your Kiss I taste
Your touch I feel each time I hold the hand of another
And your Breath I breathe
I'll never be free.

You are the spring of my winter, sun of my moon,
Your smile is the warmth that melts frozen whispers
Thaws icy emotions releasing the man inside.

Your love is the strength that burns my heart with a fire
that takes my spirit higher and fills me with desire

And as I run marathons of tip-toed desperation
I cry...begging God to let me find you again
But here I am...still waiting for you.

Faith

One believes
That believing becomes our reasoning
But as life and death succumb to the sounds of night and day
We pray for freedom to be FREE!

Flight be redeemed in defiance of
Murphy's Law
As tears skate along the edge of lifelines.
Circling eyes devoid of logic and language
Curse a silence that refuses to sleep

But as freedom rips free of being
Souls slip from their bondage
Faith flourishes stronger than now
Greater than this moment
Fueled by a power
Higher than the breath of being free

THERE

In a field full of roses and memories
Destiny beckons us near
Wrapped in a rainbow of harmonies
I see you there.

Foolish I was to caress thee
A wild moments weakness we share
Careless we bow to the fantasy
But do we dare.

Helpless I reach for your melody
Caught in the eclipse of your stare
Still so much more than a mystery
Didn't mean to scare.

Seeking I search for a way to see
A woman, a diamond so rare
All we have are whispers of dreams to be
And I miss you there…
I miss you…

MIJOS FUSION
Presents

Fort Worth Poetry Slams

A Poetry Slam & Open Mic Night

Every Tuesday Night

Live @ Mijos Fusion 1109 Magnolia Str

In The Hospital District Fort Worth

Free Admission-Free Parking

All Ages – All Talents – All People Welcomed

Open Mic Sign Up @ 8p

Show Starts @ 8:30p Sharp

For Info (972) 704-5001

MIJOS FUSION

National Touring Schedule

Friday Nov 7th
Kings and Queens
Oklahoma City

Saturday Nov 8th
Free The Streets
12-2
Tommy Allen Rec
Dallas

Nov 8th
We Give You Praise
Mesquite Tx

Nov 14
Standpipe Grand Slam
Lufkin Texas

Nov 15th 2014
Love Jonz Addicted
$20 Entertainment Fee
8pm -10:30pm
31 Bar and Grill BGs
3662 Camp Wisdom

Nov 20th
Open Mic Night at
Stay Cs Kitchen
8-10pm
Free Admission
6204 Cooper Str Sui 100
Arlington Texas

Nov 22nd Sat @ 5-8pm
Sik Lik Youth Poetry
Slam. TCU Fort Worth

Nov 29th
The Show
7pm
The Guild Theater
Sacramento California

Dec 6th
Comedy Vs Poetry
With Allan Stevenson
At Social Arts
Formerly Marshall Arts
8:30-10:30
106 E. Freeman

Dec 20th Flow
Ten Eleven Grill
Dallas Texas

Saturday Jan 17th
$1000 MLK SPOKEN
WORD SLAM . 7:30pm
UTA Blue Bonnet Ballroom
$15 Tickets

Jan 24th
31 Bar And Grill
The Bad Boys Of Spoken
Word. 8-10:30pm
3662 Camp Wisdom Rd
Dallas $20

Feb 14th Peaceful Vocation
Poetry slam 1-3pm
Ella Mae Shamblee Library

Jan 17th MLK $1000 Invitational @ UT Arlington
Feb 11th Peaceful Vocations @ Ella Mae Shamblee Library

That Night I Fell Into You
June 17th 1999 Nolan High School

As the sun rises, I see moons of ecstasy
shining bright in your eyes
and I can't help but wonder wet whispers
speaking spoken images
of that night I fell into you.

Baby, I remember your touch sending chills down my spine
as you caressed my mind with soft ebony kisses.

And that intoxicating aroma, the smell of roses and sweat,
made my emotions wet, a scent, I'll never forget.
I was overcome by your hunger, held captive by your stare,
a slave of mental seduction.
And as you wrote Egyptian scripture with
your tongue, you spoke
languages like Shebrew, Voodoo, Tongue Fu, Girl
I was yours and you knew.

You possessed me with the diction of a love technician
and I lost more than just my religion, I lost inhibition.

Without saying one word, you taught
me rapture, my heart you captured with teeth-mark
confessions and piercing injections of erotic perfection that
sank deeper than any erection.

Even now as we lay, I hear faint echoes rippling in the wake
of an erotic love song that only you could sing.
And oh what a sweet song.
So...before I walk away, let me just say you were my teacher
and I will always remember that night I fell into you.

Stars Are Writing Poetry

Dark skies become nightshade for the hunted.
I cry the milky-way.

The stars are writing poetry again
And I a moon-child
must listen to words woven by time.

Big words in bold borealis
Scream an epiphany in streams as they race across galaxies of discontent.

Meaningless tear-prints leave trails of stardust and sadness, deep, dark and damned where there is so much space that even the echoes are afraid to venture...

But still...the stars are writing poetry and I a moon-child must listen with my soul.

If I'd Known

Of false hopes and erotic wishes
of vultures in their respite.
Some poets speak prose tendering painful reprise
But my pen simply refuses to sketch the outline of your lies

Because this is not you.
It's just the blue goo oozing inside your thighs
And If I'd known that the heart breaks forever,
slowly dismantling itself into unrecognizable plots of misery,
If only I'd known that love leaks its sapphotic sap,
with vulgar invisibility, weaving sin into the
bedrooms of intimate strangers.

And If I'd known that loneliness could stifle joy,
loosen joints and force tongue against cheek
or that despair would confine me,
winding itself around my heart in beautiful unsettling,
And that you, with your sassy Episcopalian insolence,
your twisted sappho-sadistic expressions
and knowledge of bittersweet
bisexual delights would hurt me so.

Still, I would have loved you.
But from a distance,
I would have left your ass whole and wholly
for the delicious defecation of those
who wanted more and cared less.

If only I'd known…

On The Inside

Inside we walk toward this light that beckons us to look deeper within our being
And wonder…is it true what we're seeing?
Or is it our souls fleeing the truth of our reality?

There's a space deep inside where old memories die.
They sway aimlessly toward a pit and sit next to sadness,
This place is called madness.

In that space, our souls become so cold that it
controls our emotions. And we've all been to there…
Despair!

But while on this journey to our center, we feel the winter of melancholy as tears freeze becoming hell flakes that block our path with no expectations of what is or will be
when we finally reach our destiny.

And even though we all gather at the same place on the inside.
On the outside, we smile and pretend.
To me "that" is the greatest sin.

In Your Eyes

Each night, I am awakened by soft whispers calling me,
calling me, as winter winds swirl inside my mind,
creating heart-shaped clouds guided by love's
gentle breeze.

I am simply driven insane by your presence,
cause I've been digging' you for awhile now.
Don't you know that it takes everything I have to
contain my hunger
because my admiration is not just infatuation,
but a fixation on the woman inside.

Within your eyes, I see blue flames of fires
lit with mental match sticks,
fueled by passion's kindling
as it burns to new heights,

I want to be the man that lights your eternal fire...

Butterfly Kisses

*Your mother...earth, your father...time
Brother winds, sister rains inside
my mind.
My frown your moon...my smile your sun
Together we'll grow...together as One.*

*Seeds planted, fertilized with love
Await blessings from God above.
Hope springs eternal, as roots sprout
My child, my joy growing up, going out.*

*That twinkle in my eye is the guiding star
Tells you where I've been and where
you are.
My breath becomes the gentle breeze
That cools the aches of fragile leaves.*

*My love goes on forever and a day
Cause little blossoms would wither away.
Petals would dry on brittle stems
Baby, I'm the tree, you're the limb.*

*If ever I needed a single wish
I'd wish for a butterfly's gentle kiss.
Snatch time by the hand of another day.
And keep you safe, from harm's way.*

*In twinkling eyes, hope dances
Tears water seeds of chances.
Seasons change, tilled by time
Spirits grow in fertile minds.*

*At that glorious moment your
flowers bloom.
I'll be watching by the light of a bright
full moon.
Thanking God for granting wishes.*

Violation

Tonight, she fondles herself with imagination as she lies there next to me.
I am awake in her slumber, stepping ever so softly so as not to stir
the demons that taunt her daydreams as she screams out his name!!!
And as I walk the path of past men and their foreign tongues,
I wonder will she ever see me standing there?

For now, she sleeps only to be awaken to the cries of children living
in between the cracks of walls that speak the old testament of project
buildings, while those, denied tomorrow, haunt time in yesterday's
laughter leaving her to mumble old Negro spirituals.

And as she stumbles in mid-sleep,
tossing and turning in memories of nothing,
she searches the shadows of a distant reality to find a precious virginity
taken at the height of midnight by a drunken relative
But this type of violation is done on a daily basis
far from teenage fantasies and Cinderella fairytales,
far from little red riding hoods as its written
by those who lack proper menstrual penmanship

Lust is just a four-letter key used to unlock
forbidden pleasures of hidden treasures with inches of sick wisdom
But this is how some men measure their manhood
"FORGIVE THEM FATHER" for they know not what they've done

And even though she tries to separate herself from fantasy and reality
she still chooses sex over romantic notions
and her sun simply refuses to shine

For now she'll continue to fondle herself with imagination

Perhaps I'll try to move the moon again tonight
But I know she will never see me in any other light

NEW BEGINNINGS

Nothing grows beneath the feet of old sorrow when trampled by the Attila of tomorrows.

Nothing grows beneath a morning sun betrayed by the wings of dusk. Nothing…but bitter weeds of disbelief entangled like night vines strangling every inch of my being.

It's sadistic stems spread out in every direction as they eat away at spaces usually reserved for love...for life.

And there's no escaping the need to remove the weeds that choke the sun and devour the hours of days. And there's no escaping the truth that trust forgot. There's no need for that…None.

But I've already sliced too much from the edges of myself to fit her image. I've already sacrificed the fruit of my soul…to be the apple of her eye and…
I've already circumcised so many of my beliefs to make room for her moon, so that I could feel her seasons, and embrace that cold cruel touch... she called love... I've already lost too much.

And all that's left...is this fragile frame weakened by the frost from her winter. Unless…I can somehow peel back the skin of my soul and til the soil of this emotion…yard by yearning yard, the sap pouring from the pores of yesterdays will drown my tomorrows and make it where I may never become strong enough to breathe on my own again.

So here I sit, waiting for the wind to chase away old reminders and my garden becomes green and forgiving. I wait and pray for the strength to clear away the shrubbery so that I may water the soil of my soul with the gospel of poetry and cultivate a New Beginning in me.

Because I do not wish to rely on old reminders mired in the moor of memories to get by. And soon…perhaps tomorrow…my heart...will love again.

When a Man Cries

When a man cries...
It is a process that begins from deep within his soul
and takes hold of all he was and will be.

His tears form a kaleidoscope in the dark
As he embarks on a journey toward the light.

But like roots being torn from the earth
his heartache rips at the night
as he fights to hold back the flood of emotion,

But...he can't hold back the emotions.
Because he's not that strong.

So the bow breaks and he begins to shake.
His eyes, still, quickly fill with rivers until
He no longer sees...the need...to be.

But if you venture close enough,
You just might see the little boy inside his eyes.

And if you sit long enough
You just might feel the rhythm of shadows
Dancing near his tears.

And if you happen to open your mind to this moment
You just might hear him moaning in shades of blue.

Chocolate Kisses

Slipping...Sliding in chocolate hazes
Dipping...diving in sugar dazes
My donut glazed...my tip ablaze
How I long for sips of your Milky Ways

I only needed Reeses reasons
To taste the taste of chocolate seasons
To sniff wild cherry it's smell so pleasin'
To taste the Hershey touch of teasin'

Come pour yourself a cup of me
Liquid emotion stirred with ecstasy.
Brittle Skittles little bites and nibbles
of sinful gems and M and Ms.

Mr. Goodbar in Mounds of Almond Joy.
Juicy Fruits, Babe Ruths and Chips A Hoy
Crunching...Munching with all I've got.
With Krispy Kremes and Red Hots.

Desperately clinging to coco dreams
Flooded moments of Toffee screams
Mingled bodies...melted wishes.
Chocolate is the taste of kisses.

Giselle's Writing Workshop Poem #2
Things worth saving.

Souls, memories, time, money, space, trees, antiques, bonds, disk drives, gas, youth, chivalry, newspaper clippings, phone numbers, model cars, my daughters perception of a good man, old emails, books, old DVDs, CDs, tapes, the Bible, daylight, childhood, ideas, paper, passwords, pictures, depictions, scriptures, encryptions, all the negative shit people say daily and use it as motivation, good friends close, enemies closer, me, you, him, her, us, we, them, lives one poem at a time...

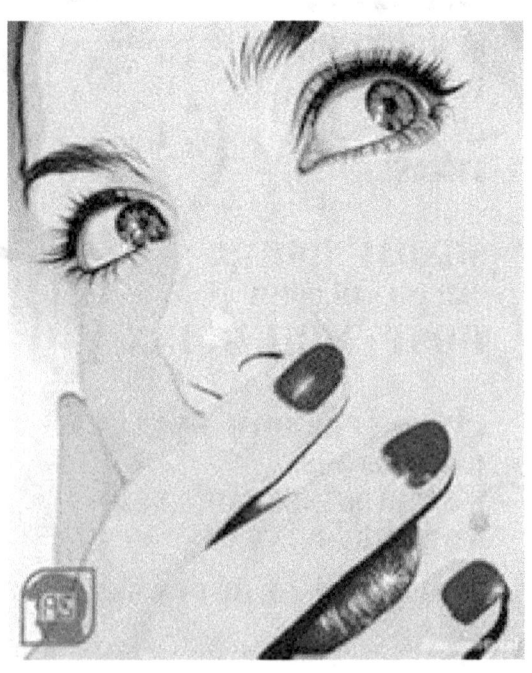

I'm Ready

You know I've already made all the mistakes a man can make trying to find the love of my life. And its been more than a million fantasies since a real woman last kissed me...And this heart is still mending. Now what I need is someone who speaks tenderly, renders me tipsy with whispers. Someone with whom I get lost in the acoustics of her smile as I listen to the music of her voice and have no choice but to simply give in. I surrender. And I wish I could describe how much I need you, and every night I get down on my knees and beg God to send me someone just like you. Cause all I want to be is that neo soulja giving in to the warrior within cause I can't do this without you. Without you girl...It where are you? And now that I've sacrificed the fruit of my soul to be the apple of your eye, I stand here faced with the decision to either run or fight for that revolution behind your eyes, because I want you to see me as so more than just a big dick with good credit. Woman don't you realize that I would kiss you sunshine, love you sunsets til your silhouette gets wet just to spite the angels. And girl you better believe that there ain't no vibrators in Heaven, But I'd gladly be your vibrator right now. It would be my honor. Tell me how can two drums become one when our sun runs from the dawn and how in the hell can my Africa survive without you. Don't you know that I would sin for you, give up grin for you, and if rhythm was the sun, I'd blend into you. Just to taste the hot sweet chocolate of your sticky satisfaction. I'm ready, Ready to be me for you so that we can two brand new. I'm ready for you to move me, soothe me and if I poot, excuse me.

Now I know that may sound silly but I'm being completely realistic. You see I've already wasted enough time molding me into the mandingo I was born to be. You see I'm ready to be your psycho gynecologist, a para vaginal orthodontist, a certified clit technician. Cause this tongue here is on a mission. To flip you in positions that leave your girlfriends wishing they knew voodoo so that they could swap places with you. And oh the pussibilities. Now I know I may not be the king or your dreams but I am the prince of potential. And I'm ready. To walk the dog inside me and never bring his ass back. I'm ready to go where no man's gone before because YOU deserve that. I'm ready to go where no mans ever gone...Your soul...And I'm ready to go.

I'm ready for love, I'm ready for life, I'm ready to make you my wife...I'm ready and I'm waiting.

Look. My name is Michael...I like football, watching Lifetime and Jesus. My favorite color is blue and just like you...I'm looking for love too. And it would be so nice to shine inside again...But I can't do that without you...I'm ready...Y'all. I'm ready...

The 10th Annual King and Queen of Erotica Poetry Slam

LIVE AT THE URBAN CAFÉ

1500 Jackson Street Dallas Tx

Saturday Sept 24th 8:00PM -10:30PM

GUIDED BY MIKE GUINN

A Sexy - Sensual - Safe Sanctuary

THE MOST EROTIC POETRY EVENT THIS FALL

$200 CASH

Only $7 In Advance. $10 @ The Door
Music - Great Food - Wine - Atmosphere...
Featuring The DFW's Hottest Singers-Comedians-Poets
Contact Mike Guinn Ent For Tickets (817) 412-3964
www.mikeguinn.com

MOIST

Sometimes I miss you so much, that I wanna just kidnap your image from my dreams and hold it hostage in my arms forever. Perhaps it's because you move as smooth as Saturday's shadow with a smile like Sunday morning...as amazing as Janeans's style.

You Are Every Woman!

You remind me of a beautiful tragedy, tragically magical, and as mysteriously unpredictable as a southern sky behind partly cloudy eyes. And I...never know when you're gonna to rain or shine. But you know what...I can't wait to get wet. I wonder...if I leave daylight at your doorstep and bathe you in springtime will the seasons become you?

If I cultivate kisses of never ending rhythm from the twilight of my eyes and... plant rainbows between YOUR thighs...will you grow Jill Scott's Afro inside? Cause I don't wanna just lift up your dress and make a mess with hot sex.

And I refuse to devour all the moonlight in your midnight til the sun sets.
Ah hell NAH! That would be too easy.

But for ONE night, your nipples, will become tic tacs for nymphomaniacs bold bald and black. And I'm just 6 kisses from that soggy sin-sation THERE! WHERE? THERE!

And all I have to do...is follow the goose bumps to the gospel of your G-SPOT and leave HALELUJAHS in the HUSH...of your thighs...WHY! Because I can.

Woman I'm just 2 numb thumbs from licking you another language. Alla-walla-way.

And when I'm done, teasing all the right reasons...you'll need a day planner to organize the orgasms and a road map to keep track of the spasms. There! Where? There?

And ain't nothing I wouldn't do for you, hell I'd even clone myself so you'd have two.

And then we'd have a threesome, just me...me...and you.

We'll leave day-screams between bed sheets and teeth marks beneath pillows and give the tooth fairy tourettes. I'll taste your wiggles...chase your giggles til I hear you say "Daddy"

And just because I'm older, don't mean I won't bang in your white T' leave stains on your white T.

Woman I'll suck your big toe and make your pinky toe jealous.
Make vibrators stand and salute me when I walk by.

That's why I write this way, recite this way and by the end of this poem I'll bite this way. Leave you as helpless as a hummingbird without wings in a tornado of tongues.

Why am I saying all of this, because I'm obviously trying to make you...MOIST! I wanna open your mind and make you...moist,
Take the time to make you...Moist! THERE! WHERE? THERE!

Because the truth is...LOVE is the best climax the heart can ever have.
And...I know you need the same thing...I do, spiritual sunshine when it's cloudy and the soul is blue.

And in the morning when I wake beside you, I wanna smell what you ate the night before in the crease of your smile, ME! Taste the dewdrops in your daybreak and know that you are satisfied. HERE, WHERE? HERE! And when the day ends and we're lying in each other's arms again...I'll cover you in my drops, with kisses that won't stop, caress you in the right spots and I WON'T stop ...til you get...MOIST!

LOVE'S LOCOMOTION
A Conductor's Love Story

HUNU MY HEART'S CHU CHU would be a HUBU with bad billing, expensive storage charges and a flatcar full of containers filled with emotional baggage and FRAGILE FREIGHT OF ALL KIND.

Woman, your heart…seemed to always be filled with everything from fake smiles to empty promises, from fresh frowns to old good-byes. EVERYTHING…except…love…

And all I wanted, was to make the safety of your soul…my one and only destination. But I couldn't… because our passions seem to always be off track. So my goals failed…ship sailed...and this old heart…simply derailed.

And it's too bad I didn't meet your SEAL of approval…
And it's so sad that you were just a sassy CHASSIS with an attitude that would've never cleared customs.

Especially since you were so use to jumping from track to track, causing delays on rainy days...you see, you were the Queen of diversions.

But if you'd just pulled into the Hub of my love for hugs or…
If you'd just allowed me to interchange US with WE or…
If you'd just allowed me to connect spiritually and give all I had…emotionally… then my load would not be so empty…
And maybe, just maybe you and I could have ridden the Z train together, forever.

And even though I still have good billing on a shipment of moonlight and stardust, the P train headed to the heaven inside your eyes will never leave this station.

And I will never be able to deliver this symphony of train whistles and sunshine I've held in the palm of my soul all my life for you.

And all that's left...is the hope that one day you'll allow the vessel of my voice to ingate at the port of your heart with a handful of hopes and kisses. But until then…I'm no better than a hummingbird without wings…because you see…I'll never fly again without you.

Shy Compliments

Silently she sits quietly
surveying the room
Is she married or single??
I can only assume
From first glance I've noticed
her beautiful eyes
Luscious lips, curvaceous hips
are just a part of her disguise.

Her smile, hypnotic makes
for an exotic potion
As I sit I have to admit that she is, poetry in motion
Mysterious lady, so nice, so sweet
The smoothest woman,
going or coming
any man could meet.

Her presence is that of
dreamy perfection
Her image incites erotic obsession
Perhaps I'll find a way to
convey this sentiment
And tell her, she's beautiful
...my highest compliment.

Every Day

If I could capture a rainbow, I'd wrap you in my favorite colors and paint you perfect. And if you truly knew you the way I do. You'd know why I'd get down on my hands and knees. Reach inside my soul. Gather moonbeams and starlight. Arrange them in a beautiful bouquet.

*Place them at your feet and say...I grew those for you
And every day all I do is think of ways to do and say more than I did the day before. To tell you how much I miss you. And all I want to do. ALL I EVER WANT TO DO...is to taste you Tuesday, wake you Wednesday.
Quench your Thursdays til Friday
Then sit Saturday sipping your Sundays til Monday.
You see I want to love you daily.*

*I want you to get sprung in the spring
Sizzle in the summer
Feast on me falling, calling as you and I
anticipate the Autumn, and get buck wild below the
waist in winter.*

Because my love...is all the seasoning you'll need.

*I want you to go crazy as I slide off your Januarys
Pull down your Februarys, March right up in between your Aprils as your May becomes June and your July...
Lays naked in the August of my September until you remember...that October...was when my naughty November eased inside your delicious December.
Listen...All I'm trying to say is...I want to love you*
                                               EVERY DAY!

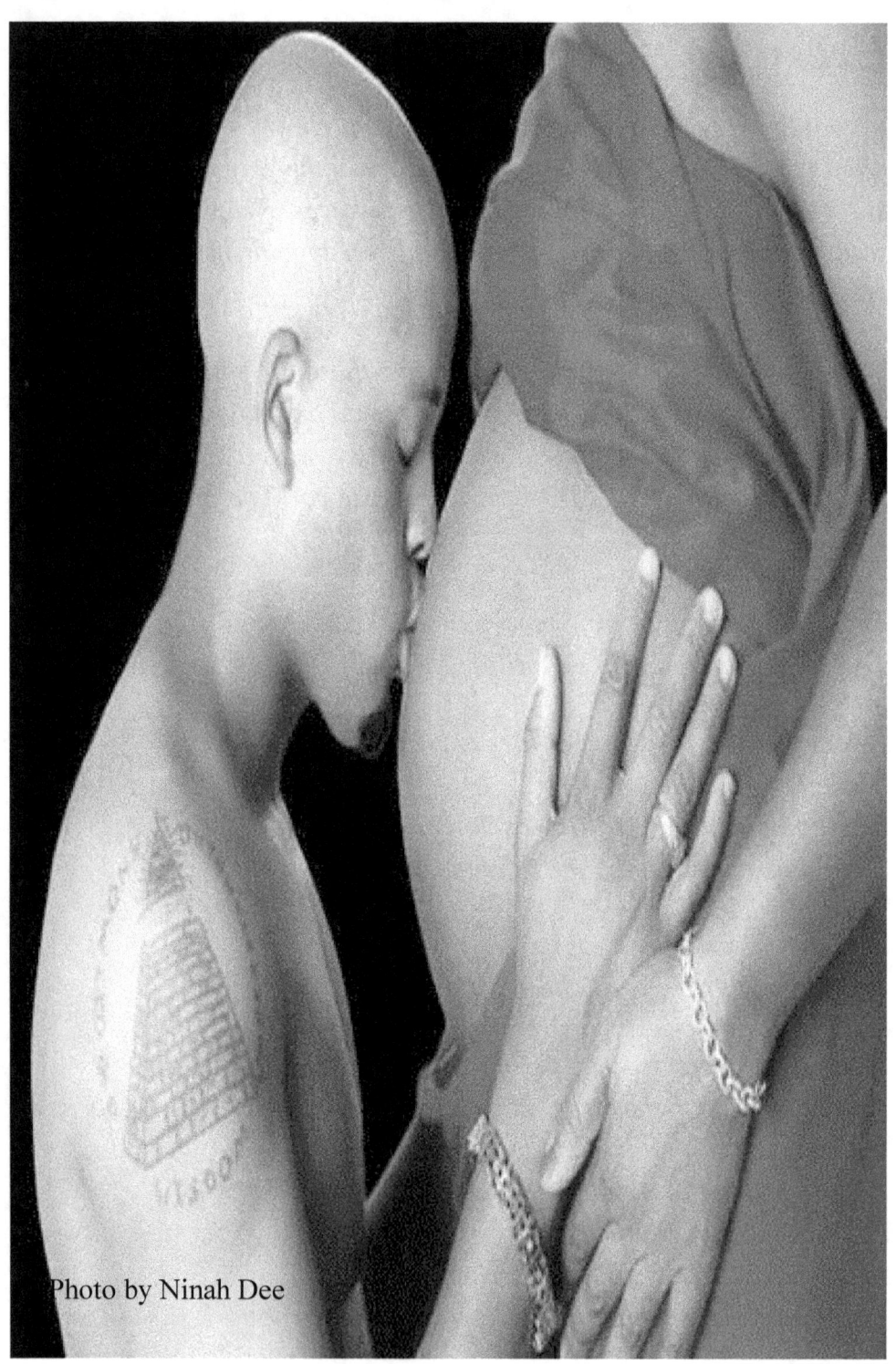
Photo by Ninah Dee

The Taste of Touch

Here...

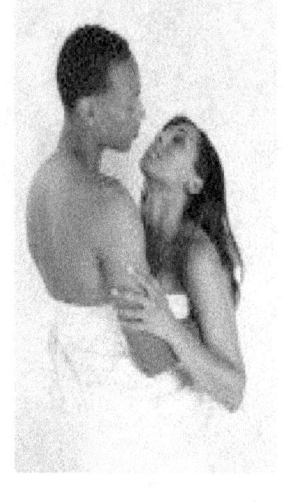

So soft the taste of skin smooth, silky
slippery, as lips slide effortlessly amid
currents of liquid emotion.

Rapidly, romance ripples across
quivering limbs drawn closer with
each gentle wave of kisses.

Burrowing hands find you trembling
there.

Where a trespass of soft caresses unfolds,
take hold, then separates
with passion unbridled.

We meld into one as emotion
heightens and embrace tightens, subduing
perfection with mental erections creating
sensations indescribable.

I'm in. Cascading slowly, through sensitive folds
of ebony. As chocolate peaks atop mounds of brown stir
constant urges to touch...to taste that Taste of Touch.

You Should Have

I wished I'd known this before
The signs were there,
But I did not care,
You should've told me I meant more

I'm suppose to recognize disguise
Your feelings weren't real
If only I'd known not to feel
I probably could've if I'd opened my eyes

If it were me I would have told you
If it were me I would have shown you
Unconditional love sent from above
If it were me I would have loved you

I wish I'd known it was a matter of time
That your heart wasn't in it,
And that your love had its limits,
You should've told me you'd never be mine

AT LOVERS ROCK
A Gypsy Serenade

I crawl inside your temple
On bended knees with baby
please on my breath.
Hoping the prayer there in
night air was fair where I'd
fine you.

Kneeling so appealing,
revealing **Gypsy serenades**
Reeling, unsensuous shades of cascading rays. How I longed to touch the shape you made.

Moonlight fidgets and fights to be go unnoticed by your affection. But color smothers color while painting your reflection.

Blue notions hide emotions that run deeper than any ocean.
But I am consumed by the power of your passionate pink potion.

Listen...Voodoo beckons the hush of the rush. As I press hard against moist moments anyone has yet to touch. I want you. I need you. Let me know how much. Cause this voyage is the lesson we've yet to discuss.

Shhhh…sun cums...Moon beams…we scream spoken words that no longer command this serene dream.
Go ahead and baptize me, then revive me in a mountain of cream.

Lips lock, ships dock at…Lovers Rock…

BEAUTIFUL

Yesterday...I shook hands with a crack addict and she stole my fingerprints.
Just a young girl in a bad world with bee stings for nipples and mosquito bites for needle marks. And still there she be...Standing on that corner.

She be like mice scrambling to hide when the light comes on.
Scrambling to hide from the sun.
It's 95 degrees in the shade and she's trying to get paid but no money she's made today.
No money she's made.

And nothing pisses me off more than to see sistahs with fever blistahs,
twisting, insisting on a ride so that they can play hide the soldier with men old enough to be their fathers, and you want to save them but why bother.
When they rather pull cock capers for paper, because nothing will save her from her ...but her.

Armed with AZT, morphine and dreams she be lean and mean...she be flying, trying to find peace in back alleys the only way she knows. But I suppose there's no hope because the only way she can cope is to tear down the temple of her body let it become a valley for viruses and dope.

But if only she knew just how Beautiful she be!
If only she'd just kick off those high-heeled blues and choose not to lose her way.
Choose not to waste her day...Because life is too high a price to pay.

But she'd rather be dressed in leather...Oh so clever
She be dressed to impress...she be the best at making less look like more
She be what she chooses, confusing losing her dignity
And spiritual virginity to men who see nothing more than a whore.

But she...doesn't have to be a midnight princess straddling fences,
bending, pretending that this is her mission in life, to lose all she was and will be in the kneeling position. Because this is not what God intended...It's not!
And she doesn't have to be feigning, screaming from the semen forever
choking her dreams...She doesn't. If only she'd realize that she....is Beautiful, Beautiful...just Beautiful, Beautiful...so Beautiful...Beautiful!

That her knees are not meant for concrete defeat
That her lips are not suppose to be that dry...
And if she'll just stand...take God's hand...She'll know...
And if she just slows down when she strolls past that convenience store window...she'll know...and she'll see that she is Beautiful, Beautiful,
just Beautiful, Beautiful...so Beautiful...Beautiful she can be.

A Poet

I must be getting closer to finding my soul mate. Because lately, all I see is her image in my dreams. You know that special someone who compliments my swerve with her verbs fills my mind with her words, defies gravity with her curves. A Poet.

Someone whose love becomes voodoo and the way I do everything from writing her name to playing games is simply taboo. The kind of woman who makes me feel so warm inside that I just want to get butt naked, run outside and try to capture the sunshine falling from her eyes. Someone who knows how to celebrate satisfaction with a reaction from her soul and understands…that her mission is not to put me in a position to make up things she wished I'd done one too many sins ago. Someone who knows just how to flow.

Ya know. And each morning when I wake beside her. She'll know just how much I care. Because it will show…in the curl of her toes, the crease in her clothes, and the kiss on her nose. And it won't even matter that she has that…morning breath, because her breath is my morning.

You see, I'm a dreamer. A man who just wants to share his heart with her heart, his spirit with her spirit, leave tear prints in the shape of ankhs so that her soul can hear it.

And at night while she's laughing, crafting izms from the day, I'll cry my way back inside her eyes until her smile becomes my religion. And don'tcha think, I deserve to have someone who won't run from the warmth of my sun. Someone who allows my will to give in to the pen in her hands as I become a man in the corner of her eyes and then die right there, over and over again until we get it right. Someone who enjoys writing my love into her life, because I'm her favorite poem.

And she can't help the way she feels she can't stop the way she is and why would she?!

And all I need to know right now is. IS THERE A POET IN THE HOUSE TONIGHT?? STAND UP!! Stand…take my hand and together you and I. We'll write rhythm, read rhymes, and make little baby wisdom's from the knowledge of just knowing what love is.

You see I'll always feel this way. Because in your hands, I'll place my hands and then our hands will become one hand holding on to forever. And whenever you need me, you won't have to look far, just glance left of moonlight, right of a falling star and there'll I'll be, waiting for your chills to catch up with the wave of Goosebumps flying south towards the summer of my kisses. And I'll always be there, not far from here where love first began as tight ass line, written in a love poem scribbled on a napkin, abandoned at the back table at our favorite restaurant, somewhere near the sweet n-low and heaven.

You see I've always felt this way…a rhythm searching for rhymes, that poem inside your mind, in love til the end of time.

Paralyzed

You told me, "One day God will reveal who we truly are." Those words may as well have been machetes slicing my heart into tiny pieces of unforgettable moments, that will forever leave me puzzled, paranoid and lonely.

My dreams are now one-way corridors leading to closets packed full of skeletons that leave me...paralyzed from the eyes down.

Now...I find myself faced with skeletons you've embraced and together with lust and lies they manipulate faith, leaving nothing but this empty space. And I...am overcome by numbness because the sum of us-we = none.

I wish I could add up all the times I'd wished I'd said something, done something, prayed for something instead of just standing there, staring into that closet watching your skeletons devour our love.
But I just stood there...PARALYZED...

Dodging the dilation of your speechless eyes, as each wink became an exclamation, with no explanation for why you refused to STAY!
Because my tears could fill the Atlantic.
And there is not now nor will there ever be a universe that could ever hope to hold all the love I still have in my heart for you.

STAY...for all the times our lips met and...
STAY! For all the laughter we'll never forget. The road trips...the parks, the poetry from our hearts...Baby...Please...STAY!
Because...You are my poetry.

And if you truly knew you the way I do then you'd know why I'd get on my hands and knees, reach inside my soul...gather moonbeams and starlight. Arrange them in a beautiful bouquet, place them at your feet and say...I GREW THESE FOR YOU.

And if you were here...right now...I'd mix teardrops into paints and cry rainbows...then I'd capture each one on canvas and create a picture that says just 3 words...I LOVE YOU!

"One day God WILL reveal who we truly are."

And maybe in the next lifetime when roses are blue, our spirits are new, us = me and you. You'll allow me to be your poetry. But for now...even your skeletons have frowns. Because without you...I'll always be paralyzed...from the eyes down...

My Favorite Flower

For each precious petal time removes,
Love grows!
From sturdy stem to terrific thorn I am torn into a million moments
Spread out in a bouquet of passionate promises.

Promises to love from my heart,
Honor with my soul, cherish with my spirit,
To give everything I have...to you!
To be committed to this fantastic fantasy called forever.

Baby, I just want to be the life-stem that compliments your
Afro-Panamanian essence.
And if you wish it, I'll love you in increments as our soul-seeds sprout
spirit leaves as fresh as the poetry in a garden of spoken words.

Please allow me to kiss your tulips
Massage your poinsettias
Surround your roots with forget me-nots
Until only my love...blooms in your eyes.
Because you are and will always be
My Favorite Flower.

Candlelight Reminds Me

Every time I Light a Candle

*Whiskey scented memories begin to burn
Inside, filling my mind with the scent of you.*

*And as I close my eyes
I think of those milky white moments
And the moon smiles with me.*

*I remember nights when two went into one,
and one between two.*

*Mathematically we fit like two square roots
multiplied to infinity
And it was just 9 past 6, when I found you trembling there.*

*A mixture of night and laughter exploded into
rush of tears and I cried too…remember…*

*But it's Ok to cry
Because I'm here and I won't stop
I won't ever stop!
Until it's time to Re-light the Candles inside you.*

Mourning

Syllables and foul vowels

scratch a trail

along my heart

like an etch-a-sketch

tracing the peaks of yesterday.

A litany of creative gestures

linger in echoes of then

leaving mouths agape

but voice is denied exit and lovers

are left to die in shades of blue.

Beaches of sandy predilection

erode from a constant pounding

simply ill-prepared for the relentless tide

of words crashing against its shore

leaving love weakened by storms refusing to subside.

That Island in Your Eyes

Love is the essence of my domain and it contains
All that I was and will be as I am and always will be in love.

But like ice melting
Tears flow in Rapids from my eyes
Flooding my aching heart.

The thaw from frozen emotions
Create waterfalls within
Without you I don't know where I begin.

Tell Me!

What have you done leaving me blue?
Loving no one…Needing you!

What do I do now?
PLEASE…HEAR MY CRIES!

I'm stranded…All Alone…"On That Island in Your Eyes."
My heart beats a tempo soft and slow,
like sad songs playing on the radio
Your kisses forsake me
Your smile eludes
Your hugs…once snug…for me…no longer choose.

So I'm saying hello again…to sad good-byes…
Stranded all alone on that ISLAND IN YOUR EYES!

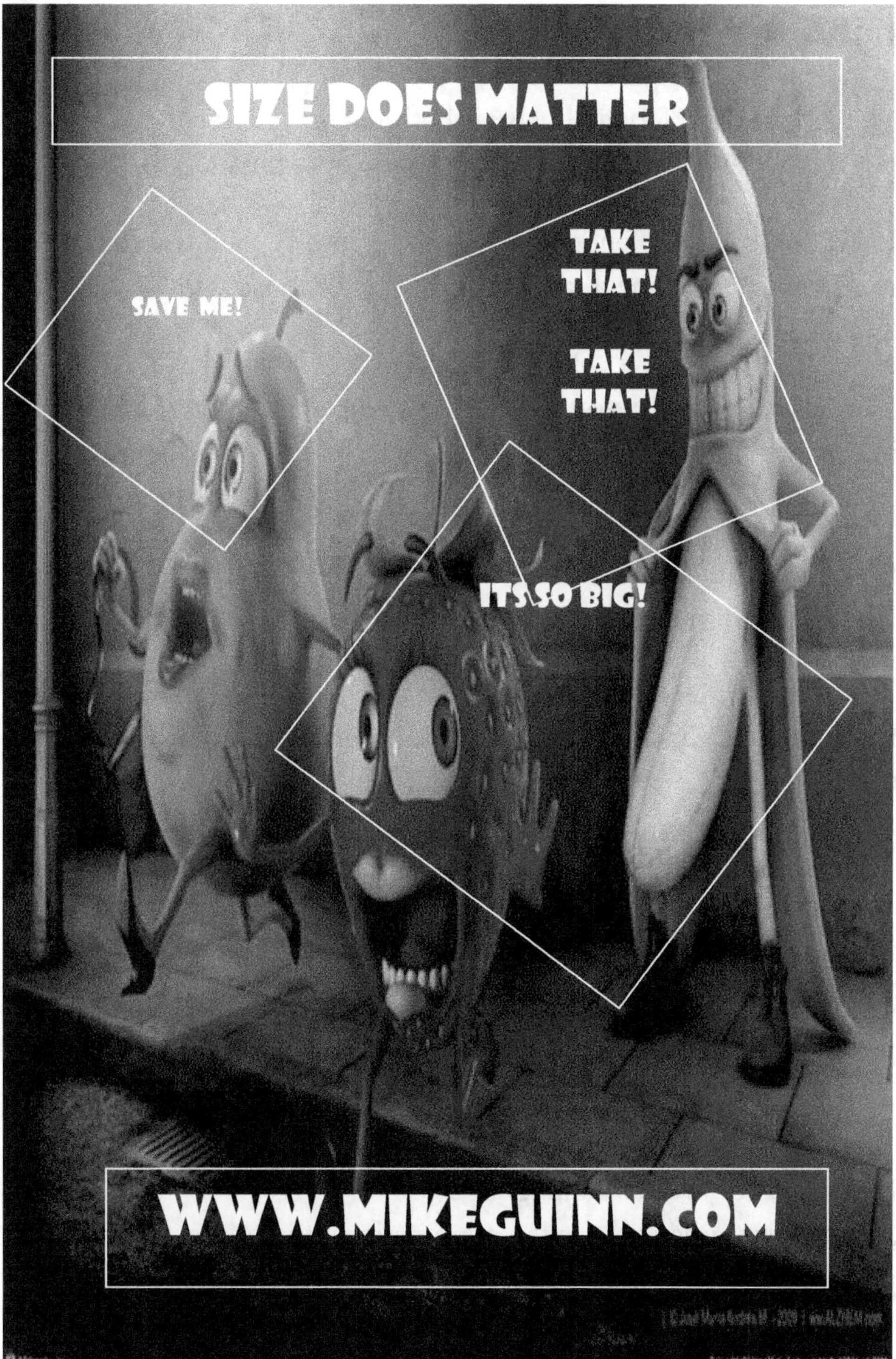
SIZE DOES MATTER
SAVE ME!
TAKE THAT!
TAKE THAT!
ITS SO BIG!
WWW.MIKEGUINN.COM

IMAGINATION...

This poem. This loquaciously titillating, slice of freedom will not be filled with selfish morals or lascivious propaganda.

Instead this benevolent example will reclassify the meaning of integrity and become a syllabus of hope for those with IMAGINATION.

There is no need for you to be frustrated because nothing but love, integrity, faith and peace should fuel the fire of even the most apathetic.

No matter life's little nuances, you have to approach your future with blonde ambition.

Sure you will face crisis and dilemmas.
But you got to be a beast. Passionate even when your eyes are cloudy.

Willing to disregard heartache's oppression to achieve pure happiness. Stop procrastinating, trust me…there will be plenty of candy at the end of your college rainbow.

Be the beauty you seek. Be a leader for the weak.
Share your space Look your future in the face.
Listen…even the sublime can overcome hatred and anguish.

If you master loves true language.
Just stay inspired and use the conjunction of intelligence and perseverance to solidify your future.
All you have to do is use your IMAGINATION.

Centric

*Transient circles
   of night and day,
      become a circumference of green earth
         diluted by shades of blue sky
      Eternity without an identity,
becomes lost in a kaleidoscope of black and white.*

*Eyes empty deny light
   flowers refuse to bloom
      time splits into metaphors
     seeps into pores
    seeking entry where
darkness first began.*

*Skin erupts into colors
   and a universe is born within.
      Gray skies speak in
         luminescent trilogies,
    raging like
a million red rivers before.*

*A moment's kiss,
   a second's bliss
      and a millennium
         blazes on in ion increments.*

*   At the blink of an eye,
   adventures glean
in tunnels of forever
Shifting in galaxies of infinity
 Life comes full circle...*

*   ...and circles never end.*

tcu joins the global effort to

STOP VIOLENCE AGAINST *women*

Join us as we raise funds & awareness to end violence against women & girls.

V-Day TCU 2012 Campaign Events to Stop Violence Against Women and Girls | March 5 – 10

Monday—*Read My Lips Poetry Slam* 6 – 8 BLUU Lounge, first floor

Tuesday—*Self-Defense Demonstration* 7:30 with TCU Police Officer Pam Christian Beck & Geren—3rd Floor BLUU

Wednesday—*Screening Tapestries of Hope* 7:30 BLUU Auditorium

Thursday—*Fundraising Night* 5 – 8 Potbelly's

Friday—*Vagina Monologues* 7:30 BLUU Auditorium

Saturday—*Vagina Monologues* 2:30 & 7:30 BLUU

Further information about V-Day can be found at www.vday.org

Beginning of the End

Scented jasmine glisten like crimson rain
 As lemon colored perceptions leap at dawn.
  Lips, swollen from soulful silence
   Swallow dew in a metaphor of shadows.
   And all who taste bow to its rhythm
    The bittersweet essence of time.

Lips, swollen from soulful silence
 Swallow dew in a metaphor of shadows.
 And all who taste, bow to its rhythm
  The bittersweet essence of time.

As flaming moments set fire to time,
 Bright lights burn in a reflection of rain.
  Minutes command seconds in rhythm
   As darkness withers from cremation's dawn.
    Empty moments creep in hazy shadows
     And time becomes a coffin of silence.

No need to fear the might of her silence
 Her passion is but a reminder of time.
  But even as she hides from crawling shadows
   Stolen moments deny the coming rain
    And peace be not still in her dawn
     For midnight refuses refuge to rhythm.

But without day, there would be no rhythm
 Memories would cease in silence.
  Here, there, misty colored teardrops become as fresh as dawn,
   Resting in fractions of time
    Waiting to murder memory with black rain.
     And thus begins the might of shadows.

Cautiously she stalks me in these shadows
 As I bide my stride in rhythm.
  Madness confines anxious rain
   Using the wind and seasons as weapons of silence.
    And while nightingales rest wings on hands of time
     Her loathing sprouts contempt at dawn.
      Here she comes again, cursing the dawn

Sister death on winged shadows.
 Perhaps eternity will grant me a second chance at time
  Maybe I'll be blessed with the stroke of her rhythm
   But if not, I'll simply weep in silence.
    Cry in colors and spew sonnets in the rain
   But if not, I'll simply weep in silence.
    Cry in colors and spew sonnets in the rain
     As certain as dawn, succumbs to rain.
      As deadly as the silence of shadows
       Time will always steal my rhythm.

Boo-ku's

Last year I lost love
And with it a part of me
Please return my heart.

Shackled ignorance
Bare feet bare witness O' Lord
Grant me wisdom's key.

        Yesterday is gone
        And tomorrow is present
        Where did the time go?

        Broken heart refrains
        Because no tears remain and
        Eyes refuse to cry.

        The trail from old tears
        Flowing down ebony cheeks
Leave tracks for kisses.

Blue skies in brown eyes
The bright sun rays give way to
Love on a clear day.

Within your rivers
Flow bubbling brooks of lust
How I long for sips.

Of Seasons Before

Mesmerized by cool reminders
shadows tumble from treetops
creeping in crimson horror
and I become a slave to dusk.

Paranoid I try to hide from autumn
but I'm too weak to move now
instead, my feet cling to this moment
like the leftover colors of spring,
while silence settles into summer's ashes
next to nowhere, close to never.

Tonight we become SEASONS,
emotions clawing at the moon
smiling east of one-way nights
crying west of morning's past
trespassing on winter's property.

So strange this moment
That tempts time with a flicker,
awaken eyes with sight newborn
so love can flourish in full bloom.

There is no why to what we do now
because becomes a reason to be
and we fall in love with the SEASONS all over again.

Afterthoughts

*Awaken by your presence
The world becomes a reverberation
filled with a mixture of space & sound.*

*Tightly nestled in soft conclusions
I search for safety in your arms.*

I close my eyes and watch the darkness become a cinema of smiles.

I've grown to depend upon the rhythm of your breath.

A cascading undulation of whispers igniting sensuous lullabies exciting my essence.

My world is complete now that my thoughts have become, cocooned in this moment.

Today, right now, and forever I live only for you.

"All Of You Cliquish, Petty, Backbiting, Egotistical, Small-Minded, Tunnel-Visioned, Nit Picky Haters Can Just Kiss My Couplet" Mike Guinn

Chosen: A Letter to My Soul Mate

(Written at the Beth Eden Singles Conference 8/14/10)
By Mike Guinn-www.mikeguinn.com

This letter, this joyfully fundamental, magnanimously effervescent display of God's Original Gift will not be a nutrageousgly grotesque representation of His grace. I'm gone keep it hood today!

As I stand here submissive to the succulent sizzle of His extravagant will. I am humbled because no matter how much I feel like giving up. I just want to give in...to you.

When I see you...I see wisdom in your eyes, the honor in your smile and I...Well, I just want to be...yours.

I may not be perfect...but in His eyes, I am perfect for you.
My dedication will set a new precedent for respect and honor.
I promise a lifetime full of intrigue and Jesus.
I love you! Your strength has commandeered my devotion.

Don't you know that the air bends beneath the weight of your quiet smile, that this Despicable me is incomplete without the essence of you!

Together we are golden, exquisite examples of summertime happiness. So let's do the right thang. I'll be your Solomon if you'll be my Sheba.
Now, I know mathematically I may not be this charismatically debonair picture of productivity.
But I have good intentions, not to mention that I offer you...myself.
So Here I am...often inadequate but willing to let go and let God because He made you.

I promise no rejection, surreal obedience, passionate initiative, and blessed endurance... my heart...To all the queens of this earth. Pretty soon the layers you reveal will take on a texture that only your true soul mate can soothe...be safe on your journey to the sun... Look, I'm no karate kid, but when I get married, I'll know why I did. Cause this is not just unabridged jargon from a wannabe playa who can only promise you pizza.
The truth is we were chosen.

Sincerely...
The Man with the Broken Smile!

MY SECRET LITTLE FANTASY
By Michael Guinn

She comes to me…in the wee hours of the morning, making her nightly subconscious booty call.

She waddles up to my bed like Mr. Poppers penguins and summons my soul with that sweet sexy smile and I just melt…
Her hair shiny, eyes like squinted little windows, cheeks pleasantly puffy, booty proportioned like my own miniature buffy the body!

Her hands…plump little dust muffins, skin soft as moonlight. And as she wraps her right leg which is a little shorter than the left one around my rock hard spirit. Overwhelming me with sheer energy.

Kissing me with her light, riding me with those robotic little hips. Faster and faster til I…I…I…I cum to realize that…
I'm in love…with this extraordinary, imaginary midget. She is the original ompaloompa, with chocolate factory thighs that makes my willy wannawonka…
Even at 3 feet 9 inches she is was and will be more woman than all the women I'd ever known. Will ever know…
Love is limitless…Time to change the sheets…

Giselle's Workshop Poem # 4
A HARD HABIT TO BREAK!

A HARD HABIT TO BREAK!

Watching Porn, midget porn like, the Wizard of Oz, Willy Wonka, the Discovery Channel pygmies, National Geographic pygmies, oh and eating short cake...

Giselle's Writing Workshop Poem #3
Inanimate object as an uninvited case…

There you are again staring me straight in the face, pointing that little crooked hand of yours at my heart. Stop rushing me and constantly…reminding me with that smug look on your face that I'll…be dead soon.

I can't go anywhere and you not be there…laughing at each gray hair, giggling in between each wrinkle…you arrogant son of a bitch. I can't stand you…

I wished you just get the hell out of my life. And no matter how much I try to stay ahead of you…**you are always there.** Boy If I were a younger man, I'd whoop yo ass….but you're too strong for me now…and each day I feel your presence growing and growing…

I tried to reason with you by eating healthy, not smoking, safe sex, church and yet you are…fucking unrelenting…you win…for now…

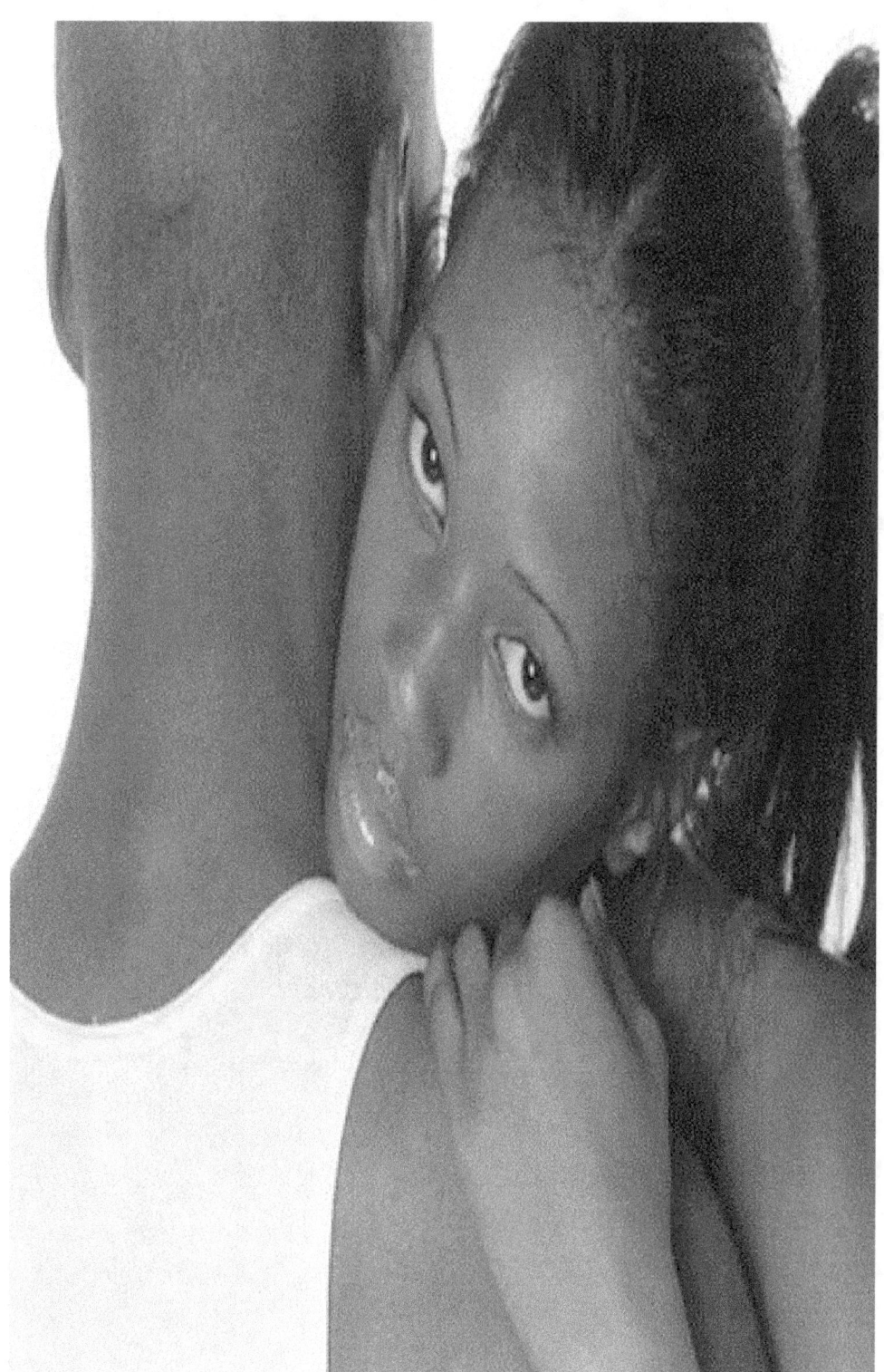

Shades of Day

You awake to the sound of day,
Gloom's viciously cloaked reminders

become Illusive, ghastly shadows,
Ill-tempered as tornado's before.

Time engages in an assault of color
As life daydreams in shades of gray

And the future becomes red slaughter
Beckoned from eve's fruity appetite,

Astute blues relent rage,
Oblique in rainy tranquility,

Sunshine sheens juicy repent,
slothing acquiesce of rebellious rays,

The reluctant tolerance of blushing cheeks
beseech bold and bright compositions.

Tiel disguised in meadow green,
skulks dusk like praying mantis.
And now these shapes,
A cataclysm of insignificance,
slight the dawn of man
defying existence in tints of time.

Without You

Without you
Silence is raped by thunder
lightning steals quiet from the night.
Bare feet become burdened by memories
of a fear that grabs the soul, chokes sound, denying life within
leaving clinched eyes grimacing from
painful reminders of days gone by.

Stitched lips simply refuse to speak yesterday's lies
as tongues hunt for helpful hints
cheek and teeth conspire to stifle
the truth of moments bare.

A heart is hardened by paralyzing silhouettes
unable to cope with crippling despair
I refuse to be half of a whole that has no half to hold
I can't go on this way,
I won't go on this way,
I can't go on this way without you

Shattered Glass

Beauty of raindrops
The essence of snow tops
The strength of time

Melancholy lament is captured in an opus of
Echoes and box springs
Whispers of bitter sweet drama from the night before

Mockery of smiles and smirks
Gesturing cool commands
As moans lie hidden in winter's pillow

Secrets become pieces of broken glass
Which the breath of life has passed through
And left shattered in a million requiems
Falling
Fading
Breaking
Refusing to grow
To breathe
To sing
To dream

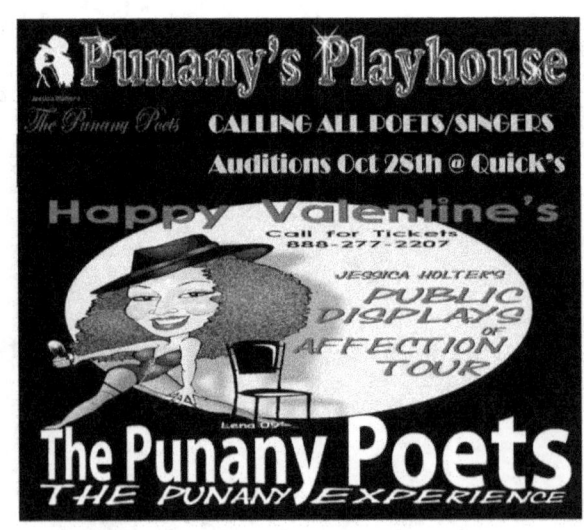

A Stranger in Your Eyes

*Minutes, hours, day pass
But that look I'm so used to, refuses to return to your eyes*

*Evolutions revolve in revolutions of unresolved resolutions
But time is the selfish keeper of what used to be a symphony*

*Poetic revelations be told in cool beats
Smooth like fat grooves no longer lean
My soul in a song*

*And even though, the shadow from my blackness
cast silhouettes all over the room
you are still so un-aware
That I'm...even...there*

*In your absence I've become engulfed by a revolution
of silence
Swallowed by the night
Lost in this moment
A prisoner to a memory*

I'm just a slave to love's cliché

*Passion refuses to caress ebony with its touch
Whispers curse the notion
As black rain drips blue pain
leaving yesterday's tear-prints on my now
and my heart becomes a place without light*

*I no longer want to taste your hyphenated kisses
I refuse to respond exponentially
To the undeserving swerve of your smile*

How dare you do me this way?

*Mystics guess and psychics confess
That they cannot see me in your future
and this prediction sheds light on the rhythm in your lies
And I see you for the first time*

*If only it were not so
But I see you now
I see a Stranger inside Your Eyes*

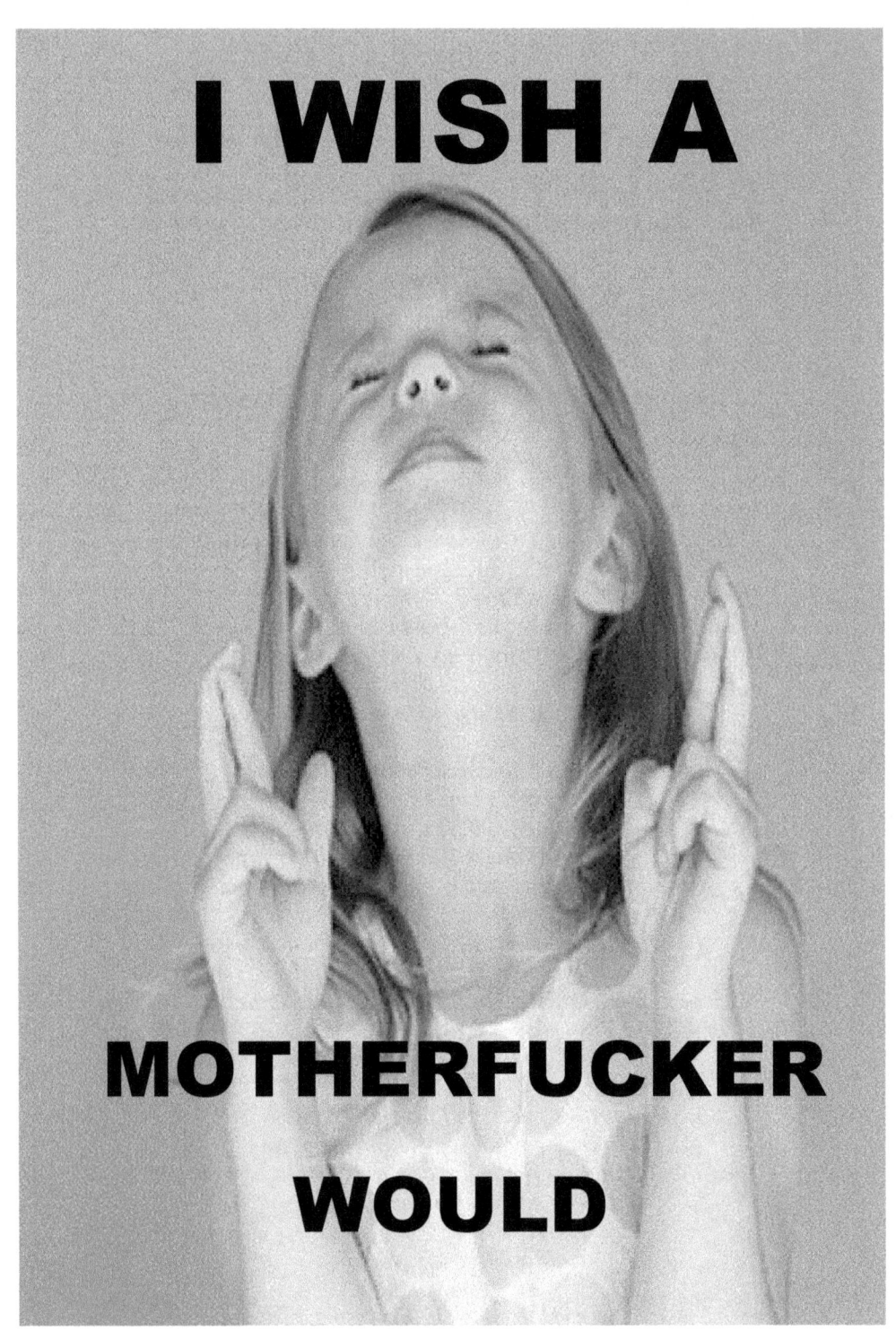

Babe, I seen you dressed super nice, I seen you in your school clothes, I seen you naked, I seen you with your sweat pants, hair tied, chilling with no makeup on, I've seen you cry, smile, laugh, mad, I've seen you sleeping, wide awake, hyper, mellow. You were always the same beautiful girl.

Blue Interludes

Confined between sheets of song,
Music spills lyrics like liquid spirit absorbing chills.

Even then no masterpiece becomes of my separated self.

Stale lines steal minutes from my life as a familiar form takes shape, distracting me from my task with incessant banging and clanging on the bars of her paper cage.

The ink destroys and recreates my thoughts as wills collide in a fight for survival-hers for release from a shallow prison of pages mine for the return of my sanity and relief from the chaos she wages.

As minutes become hours, I press on knowing I must prevail.
Words distort themselves into a cryptic smear seen through the sting of my tearful stare.

Approaching desperation, I write without care for rhythm or form.

The reflections pouring from my pen reveal nothing of what rages within.

An arsenal of emotions attack from every side-wrath, loss, shame, and pain conspire against my serenity.
Still there are others I cannot own for fear they will consume what remains of my identity.

This night I envy those who sleep in peaceful oblivion to my torment.
Would that I could enter dreams where steps of faith do not lead to disappointment.

Exiled captives scream unsettling tidings demanding to be dealt with outside the bounds of this paper cage.

Sleep

You sleep to the sound
of midnight as shadows crawl in
silence, so as not to wake the
moment.

Dark meaningless shapes
ill-tempered like the ones before
creep as you snore in colorful
metaphors.

A bluish hue of quiet,
beckons the hush.

A ginger cascade of dreams,
shuffles in a fog of poetry,
Rose red surrender,
Restless acquiesce,
Releasing the smile
of wide foreboding.

Brownish gray
describes the morning.

Day comes, night leaves,
sun shines and sleep creeps
no more.

Shallow the Water

Standing in a pool of tears
I question my feeble existence.
Often it is this weakness
that denies me life.
In limbo my soul remains

Stillness cries out in waves
As tears force emotions to compliment the mood.
Waters rise meter by moon
Essence becomes a prisoner of circles
And now eyes become rivers run dry.

Life is captured by time
held hostage by night
consumed by sound
Just a moment that quickly fades away

Now my revolution, denied
Evolution, declined
Reincarnation becomes my soul's resilience
And Shallow Waters are Shallow no more

Love's Jambalaya

A Recipe for a Successful Relationship

Begin With a Big Bowl of Openness
4 cups Love
5 tablespoons Patience
2 cups Understanding
3 tablespoons Tenderness
1 cup Forgiveness
1 gallon Faith
2 cups Friendship
A barrel of Fun
1 teaspoon Laughter
1 cup Romance
A smidgen of spontaneity
A pinch of Trust

First your combine Love and Understanding

Mix thoroughly with Tenderness

Add Faith and Trust

Then blend in Friendship, Forgiveness and "please" be Patience

Next, stir in Romance and have fun with it

Sprinkle with Laughter and Spontaneity

Then bake with Sunshine, let cool by Moonlight

Serve daily in a Dish of Passion.

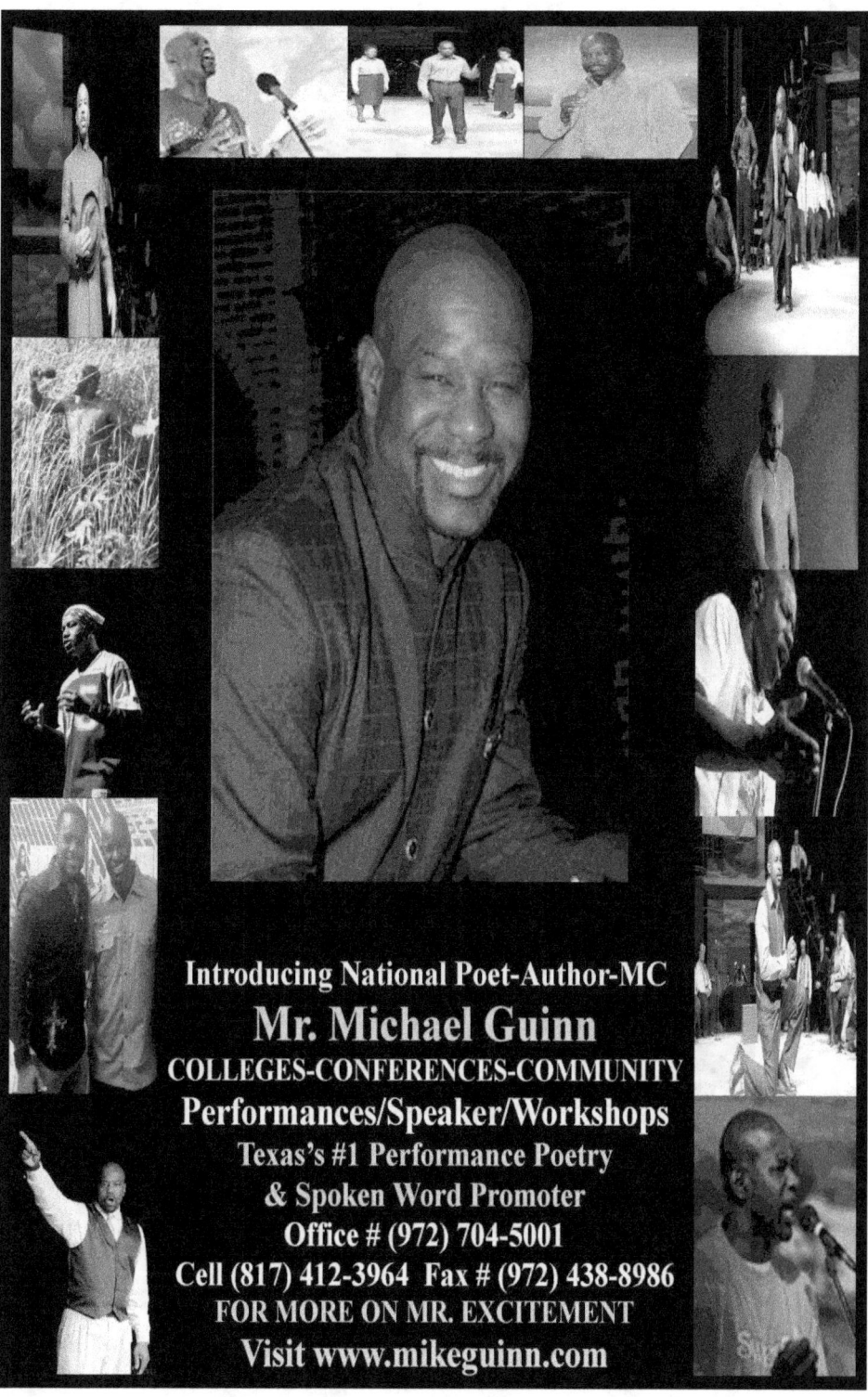

An Angel's Halo

There's a place just left of the rising sun
Where women and theology linger
Wearing hats in shapes of more than one
Fixed with delicate fingers

Nestled in bright congregations of color
Against clouds of cotton moments
Beseeched with blackness big and bolder
Their splendor pay boastful homage

Proud crowns, perched upon brown
Illuminate the day with style
Like the brilliance of colorful sound
Shades of red, in shadows of now

What a site to see, come shouts of glee
As the preacher turns to thee
"Sistah I sho do like that hat"
Grinning, from chin to knee

Their beauty shrouds day with wisdom
Mesmerizing time with light
Like an Angel's Halo, its blessed vision
Brings the wonder of miracles and might

Saints whisper gossip at the skies
While truth sermons sizzle at the brim
And heavenly melodies weep from eyes
Wrapped in tears of swaddling hymns
"Cause Sistah I Sho Do Like that Hat"

May I

May I be your Midnight in shining Armor?
Rescue you from emotional distress
Aid in your escape from lonely dungeons?
May I?

Please
Let me slay that dragon inside your heart
with just one soft kiss...
and make your soul the castle of my deepest affection
May I

And If you'll
just come with me tonight my queen
I promise that the thunder you'll feel
will not stop until the sun returns to your eyes

So please...
May I

End Domestic Violence

The Color of Misty Blues

Tangled in a cornucopia of song
Horns blow a breath of fresh air
Like Billie crying colors of misty blues
That breath was "YOU"

You be that shade of night
Dark as jazz shadows against the moon
Teasing time with pieces of a dream

Girl you are so "saxxy"
Your smile is like a sudden rush of music
Sung in tones of astrology
Like a century of forbidden whispers.

And the setting sun simply delights like slaves
freed from a summer of trumpets when you're near
Baby the rain that falls here, begins and ends in your eyes
It begins and ends with you.

If only there were a way to capture night or
corral the day.
Night and day would belong to you
And music, would collide with echoes in the wind
Like the color of Misty Blues.

Silhouette

For Marissa P.

Against the shadow of my memory
I saw your figure carved in tear-prints
Molded by fingertips, etched in my mental
With a stroke, so sharp and so deep
I could hardly breathe

Please allow me to be that moment you seek
Because I'm tired of conceding bits of me
Love me, right now, please...hear my cries
My heart is yours if you'll open your eyes

While looking for me, I've searched for you
Listened for love in skies of blue
Been hoping forever, with each sunset
Waiting for a glimpse of your silhouette

Tell me
Where can I find you, when will I know?
Hold me right now, hush don't cry
Been hoping forever, with each sunset
Because my love is yours if you'll open your eyes.

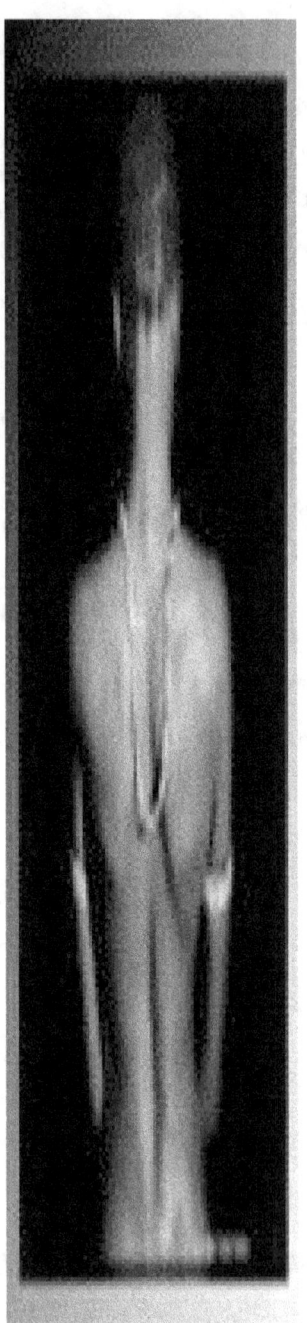

We Made Poetry
By Felicia O and Michael Guinn

(MIKE) Seductively she speaks to me…passionately pondering my intentions. Not to mention that look in her eye for a guy wanting to be the apple of hers. Well…at least the seed of her need. But she…doubted my sincerity.
(FELICIA) Should have seen the way he looked at me, or should I say devoured me with that stare, searching here (Move hands toward Chest) and there… *(Move hands down the rest of the body)* Hello…Up here! *(Point to eyes)* but his fear…was too clear, at least he was sincere.
(FELICIA) He was driving to Texas through Fresno. **(MIKE)** Yep...I was driving to Texas through Fresno.
(FELICIA) Even though it was way out his way. **(MIKE)** She invited me to stop in Fresno along the way.
(TOGETHER) Then we took a drive (at same time).

(MIKE) I thought she was fine. **(FELICIA)** He…was alright
(MIKE) She took the time to show me her house. She the cat and I the mouse. Had some time to kill so I hung out.
(FELICIA) He didn't have time to kill. 1:30 Am., dead cell phone, no car charger. I just felt sorry for him. So she invited me in to relax.
(MIKE) Well…I **was** tired. **(FELICIA)** It **had** been a long day.
(TOGETHER) So we decided to…lay…

(MIKE) Me on one side **(FELICIA)** and me on the other.
(TOGETHER) I hope she don't snore/I hope he don't snore

(MIKE) Nice…Covers **(FELICIA)** Watch out brother ain't nothing here to discover
(MIKE) She was as mean as a hungry baby
(FELICIA) And he was a little shady and there's no ifs, ands or maybes when it comes to me being a lady.
(MIKE) When she turned it was like poetry. **(FELICIA)** I wish this nigga'd be still.
(TOGETHER) (Ahhhh) The words still linger on the pillow

(MIKE) She…was fine... **(FELICIA)** He was kinda cute…but I didn't do nothing and that's the truth.
(MIKE) We were all alone... in this big ole bed...enough said…WHAT! She want me to lie to her make it sound fly to her…sure I wanted to sample her symphony and play peekaboo with her poetry…shoot…that's just in me.
(TOGETHER) She wanted 2 C what I C. B all in my poetry.

(FELICIA) See…told ya he/she was bold... **(MIKE)** not bold just better.
(FELICIA) What ever… **(MIKE)** Bark…
(FELICIA) So you wanted me to nurse your verse, nibble on your scribble, play scramble with your scrabble. **(MIKE)** Yea…let's DABBLE…
(TOGETHER) So We Made Poetry

Insignifiny

Passing by me...life denies my entrance
to a place where grinning sketches itch in skits,
Un-fetched reflections go matched,
and my surface is barely scratched.

Still time pauses long enough
For my essence to be captured by its light.
smoothly transforming me into rhapsody
and my existence becomes crystal clear.

Now restless moments pace with nowhere to go,
caught up in contemplation,
confined between chalked outlines,
wandering between now and then.

It's in this instance that I realize...
that I am simply a missing link in evolution

CHOCOLATE COVERED FANTASY

I'm hungry again
And right now I have this cravin that must be satisfied.
To me you be caramel flavored ebony
And edible slice of ecstasy
A chocolate covered fantasy

You got me "A-dick-ted" to your kisses
Melting like milky metaphors inside your pores
As my fingers explore, eyes adore
Tongue circles clit and you beg for more.

Hmmmmmm weeeeeee

My mouth waters from the scene of this Hershey shaped dream
Eyes beam, you scream
Together we cream

I kiss and lick and suck and kiss every slurp able inch
And as sugar canes dance inside your thighs, your punany wraps, grabs
and holds. Legs tighten, release, folds in a labiastic
lip-o-suction of eruptions oozing poetry that runs down your thighs,
dries and then blends into your skin

Inhale breathe…And let me all the way in…

I want to fill you so full of thunder that from now on, all you will see
when you look in the mirror is my tongue in your reflection.

Tongue Foo

I wanna taste the rain dripping from your frown
Running wild like rivers of sin down my chin
As it glistens sweet mocha madness
Melting winter sadness like summer's hot Tongue
May I have some?

I wanna feel African vibrations
Taste the amazing libation
Of sticky lies oozing from inside your thighs
May I?

I wanna sip from your well
Drink the story it tells
Cast spells, sniff smells
Create Heaven, raise Hell
Well…May I?

I wanna give long licks, big sticks
Tease the tip of your clit
Slow and easy, wet –n-greasy
Woman your pleasure is what pleases me.

Say like it girl, don't fight it girl
Shhhhh…too loud be quiet…girl…
Let it rain right now
As I take a bow
Cause all I ever wanted to do
Was to perform TONUGE FOO ON YOU…

Giselle's Writing Workshop Poem #1.
By Mike Guinn

There are no softer lips than the lips of a lesbian at midnight in the summer time in Dallas Texas.

Our Tongues intertwined as if they were born that way. We kissed for what seem like a whole got dam day.

And No other kiss has ever come close... see I still smell panama on her breath, Jamaica in her skin, and it is the closest to an orgasm I've ever been...

The texture of her top lip was perfect match to my bottom lip. We created hurricanes, torrential as Amazon rains...I melted, I still do...just like this. I still get high from the memory of that kiss...

Reeses Peeses

She had just put down the vibrator when I stepped from the shower. "Its ready babiee," she moaned as she spread her thighs wider...wider...Exposing that Nu Awlins Sun and that Ft Worth Moon. To her romance was mirrors on the ceiling chocolate syrup. A digital camera and a copy of Green Eggs and Ham. Which she liked read from the back. And I did... Because SAM I AM.

She want affections, she didn't care for kisses passed her navel just stiff erections double dipped in cream. Hard tips tapping the seam of her punany lips leaving trails of thick pearl drips. WELL! I've converted the perverted before but this one was different. She told me that wetter was better, that deeper was sweeter, that thicker made her cum quicker so I sprinkled kisses and spit, talked mo shit as I exercised her demons with my jelly and chocolate syrup oozed from her thoroughly massaged kitty. Now this had definitely been a pea nutty affair.
Reeses Peeses baby.
Reeses Peeses

Skid Marks

Love…
To me love is the skidmark left from shitty trails of stained affections long after emotions draws have been removed. Yeah those musty multicolored streaks of spotted foul bowel just itch at an opportunity to get up, get out and smear something.

It's too bad you didn't wipe deep enough, long enough...hard enough. Perhaps entrails from stanky tails would not have stained love's dainty little panty so heavily.

Never mind trying to fool these assholes by switching from fake ass black, red, yellow even polked dotted bikini bullshitters because the dark marks left on fruit of the loom hearts will always remain. But not to worry ladies and gentleman. Now there is hope in the form of a new skid mark remover called SKIDS AWAY! Yes with Skids Away all you have to do is apply a thin coat to one ply paper hoochies just as laxative lies kick in and the shit really starts to run.

Skids away is guaranteed to enemize their sorry asses or your money back. Not recommended for scratch and sniff addicts who may or may not use as directed. See coochie coupon for rebate.

Minutes-Hours-Days

If we could freeze time.
Will we revel in the thaw of hot embraces?
Will your sensual moans echo wet whispers of don't ever STOP?

Woman if I maintain this pose will the reward be wet agony
And will you grab me, have me slip
and slide in your liquid lucidity.

Right now, time is measured in erotic moments.
Sex is defined by hours and love is engraved
by lazy days of intense foreplay.

So may I tickle your fantasy with nipple licks as I dive and dip
tasting honey drips from round mounds as I search for cupid's
passion mark, touching only the bottom of your heart.

And when I sing my song, will you speak in tongues?
As moist emotions melt from deep feelings felt.
My manhood throbs so please…help yo self…

And if I sprinkle little kisses, will they touch your heart and mind
Help you seek til you find while suspended in time.
Through the rough bump and grinds.

Wait …rewind…cause it's MY TIME!

To enjoy the minutes-hours-days

Please Say Yes

For years I've stood at the edge of life's canyons
Cursed wind and rain and swore never to let
heartbreak find me here again.

I ran marathons of self-reflections
Swam seas of rejection
But could never elude your affections

I've sat and cried wet wishes
Fears melted from kisses
Before I realized that life without you...
I could not miss.
You left tear-prints on my spirit
When I chose not to hear it
My heart you took hold and treated like gold

Your love is the swan song
That burns my soul like the sun
Its strength binds my spirits bond
Gives me hope when there was none
With you is where I belong

If I never said I said I loved you
Its cause I didn't know how
If I never said it before...Lady I'm saying it now.
I LOVE YOU!

I should have done this a long time ago
I should have open my eyes
Stopped ignoring the signs
And asked if you'd be mine
Will you be mine...PLEASE SAY YES!

STOLEN GLANCES

By Michael Guinn

Dedicated to M AND M

She sits juxtaposed to his now.

Third eye open. Heart Full. Longing for the opportunity.

She sits... Glistening, Listening, and Witnessing his movement.

His gestures reek with the stench of temptation...

She senses it. Craves it. Embraces it.

Facebook posts have fueled the hunger to feed off each other's stare.

Subliminal seductions go unnoticed by everyone but me.

And for a moment forgets she belongs to another.

Caution thrown to winds rewind in minds caught up in Stolen Glances.

Ocular Russian roulette so intense a blind man could sense it.

I watch, he stands, she sits emotionally connected, sending eye lash Morse code with each blink.

I watch he turns, she spurns, desperately seeking confirmation.

But his hesitation divides the moment.

And now I know why there is no honor amongst thieves.

They Steal Glances seeking second chances. Rekindling fires wallowing in unspoken desires.

Reveling in the soul's labia, stroking the moment with syncopation.

Breathing, Stealing, Seething, Teething, Inhaling, Sailing Seas of Visual Ecstasy.

And I am nothing more than a peeping tom watching a Gospel stripper dance for her soul mate.

I watch him, he watches me.

She watches us, trap set like a spiritual spider using rays of light as webs to catch the gleam of his eyes.

She's only focused one prey.

And I pray. So she sits. She be Cat Burglar.

Ever aware of her surroundings and I watch them watching me, hoping I haven't seen what they both know I've felt.

And this is how it feels to be the other pair of eyes.

In a crowded room to see the scene unfold and be helpless to intervene.

We've become the most unlikely threesome.

But I wasn't invited.

They don't even know or care that I am there.

Too caught up in reflections and re connections unaware how its affecting the boundaries.

Bruno Mars plays softly in the distance now.

And this is how it feels to be third place in a poetry slam of losers.

The odd man out. The misfit who will never be able to recapture her eye.

The way he's captured her heart. Still here we are.

Watching each other waiting on the music so that we can switch seats to see who will be last one standing. And I am tired of being your punching bag.

All because I am not him. I'm tired of trying to keep the music playing with broken heart strings.

Now we suffer from Cataracts of the soul, blinded by each other's sight, pupils of ill requited love.

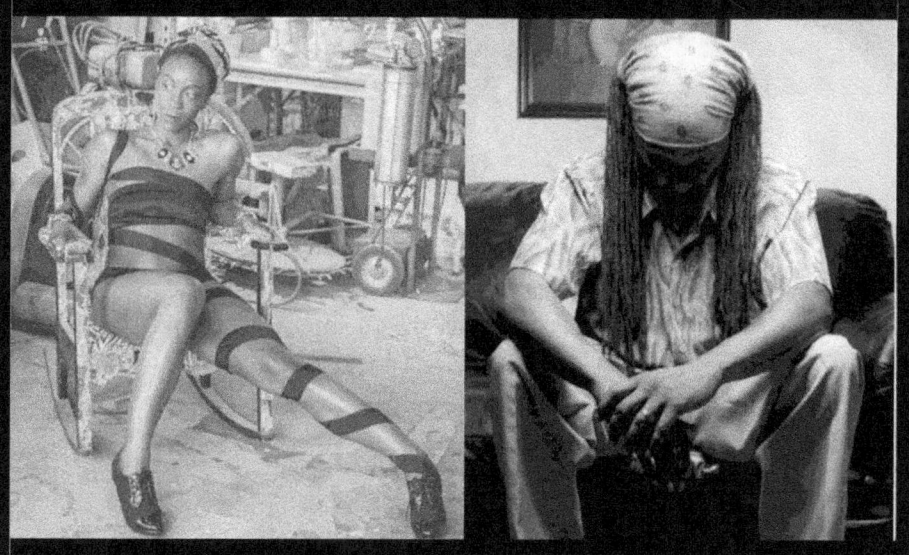

www.ingramcontent.com/pod-product-compliance
Lightning Source LLC
Chambersburg PA
CBHW050559300426
44112CB00013B/1995